ULTRA-RELIABLE
SEASONAL TRADES

by
John L. Momsen

TABLE OF CONTENTS

INTRODUCTION

Ultra-Reliable Seasonal Trades presents a collection of 41 of the most dependable and highly profitable seasonal trades the futures market has to offer. Each has been chosen, not only for its high percentage of profitable trades, but also for the foundation of fundamental logic by which it is supported.

Each of the trades found herein combines three basic concepts: seasonality, a philosophy of "mega-trades only" trading and technical entry/exit techniques. These three concepts are interwoven to produce winning trades and an overall profitable program.

Seasonal trades have the strength of history behind them. Long before there were computers to assist the trader in the formation of a profitable trading plan, there were seasonals. The major advantage of seasonal trades is the high degree of accuracy they offer. I feel that accuracy (measured as the percentage of profitable trades) is one of the most important segments of a trading plan. A trading plan may show excellent results, with a fairly low level of accuracy and a high profit to loss ratio, but would most likely require great mental endurance to withstand losses. I've heard it said that typically after three losses in a row the average trader will begin disregarding entry signals. These disregarded signals will often prove to be the profitable ones. *Ultra-Reliable Seasonal Trades* was specifically designed to avoid strings of losses. This conserves your finances and your psyche. But losses, naturally, will occur on occasion and should be expected.

The high degree of accuracy of the *Ultra-Reliable Seasonal Trades* combines with the goal of "mega-trades only" trading. I define a mega-trade as one that earns many multiples of your initial investment. Each of the 41 *Ultra-Reliable* trades is designed to place the trader in the right commodity at the right time in anticipation of mega-moves. For example, if you'd followed the *Ultra-Reliable Seasonals* September D-Mark Trade in June of 1997, you would have sold short at 5814 and covered the trade six weeks later at 5385 for a gross profit of over $5,300. A nearly 400% profit! Or, had you taken the short Heating Oil trade in January of 1997, your account would have grown by over $4,800 in only six weeks. In point of fact, had you followed all of the trades in this book from 1977, you would have made over $2,100,000 trading only one contract per signal!

Combined with the concepts of seasonality and "mega-trades only" trading are simple, easy-to-use mechanical entry-exit techniques. While seasonal trades are already highly reliable, the timing of each mega-trade may vary considerably. (I believe that the only difference between a winning trader and a losing trader is timing.) The use of precise entry/exit techniques makes it possible for the market itself to signal if and when it should be entered. You'll also find my approach often incorporates a protective stop, and in most instances a trailing profit stop.

The nickname I've coined for my personal approach to seasonal trading – which combines seasonality, technical entry/exit techniques and a "mega-trades only" philosophy – is "The Mega-Seasonals Method." It is not complicated in the least, and has proven extraordinarily profitable. Every *Ultra-Reliable Seasonal Trade* listed in this book was found and/or structured using my Mega-Seasonals Method principles. And because of its "sophisticated simplicity" I believe this book can aid – and will appeal to – all levels of traders, from rank beginners to seasoned professionals.

- Chapter 1 -

SEASONALS AND MEGA-SEASONALS

The first question we must ask ourselves is what exactly are seasonals and why are they so important?

Seasonals can be defined as the up and down trends that occur at approximately the same time every year. These market trends reflect the normal change in the fundamentals of the supply/demand equation.

To best understand the seasonals concept, let's consider the corn market. The corn market has one of the most logical and easiest to understand seasonal cycles. We will open our analysis with a look at the seasonal chart of December Corn in just a second. First, though, let me explain how the December Corn Seasonal Chart (appearing on the next page) was produced; and understand that all the seasonal charts appearing in this book were produced in a similar fashion.

The December 1977 Corn closing prices on the first trading day of each month were added. This sum was then divided by twelve to compute the average yearly price. Next, each month's price was converted to a percentage of this average yearly price. A figure of 90 represents 90% of the average yearly price. This equalizes each year's price and market climate with that of other years. The same mathemathical process was performed on each of the subsequent years of December Corn contracts. Then, the monthly prices were averaged (i.e. – all January's indices, all February's indices, etc.). This creates a monthly index number. The index numbers were then plotted on a standard X-Y graph.

Now, let's look at the seasonal chart of December Corn on page 4. You can easily see that prices tend to rise until July and then decline. This is a reflection of the normal harvest and usage patterns of the corn market. As soon as the crop is "made" in the late summer (often late July), prices begin to decline. Prices decline because the corn crop is nearly out of the range of harm from normal weather conditions (that's the definition of being "made"). We then know approximately the size of the corn crop coming to market. Remember, the markets we're dealing with are *futures* markets. The December corn prices are looking to the future and to the new crop of corn that will be marketed in the late fall to early winter period. This explains the steep drop in December Corn prices from July, even though the harvest is yet to begin.

DECEMBER CORN

1977 - 1997

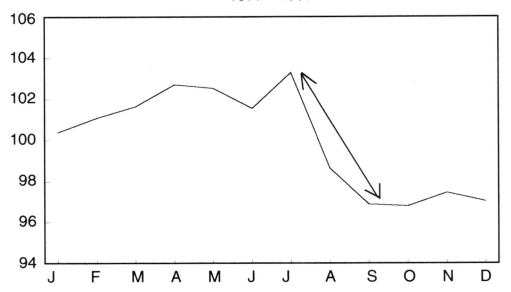

After July/August, you can see that prices tend to decline much more slowly. As the crop year progresses from harvest to the next planting season, December Corn prices tend to rally due to the decrease of corn on hand. The rally picks up steam in the June through July time period. During this time the weather has considerable influence on the new corn crop. This is called a "Weather Market." As soon as the corn crop is made, the cycle begins anew.

Remember, this is only a simple explanation of the supply/demand factors of the corn market. The number of cattle on feed, pigs on feed, crop carry-over from last year's harvest, weather conditions in other corn producing countries (many with reverse seasonals because they are south of the equator) and prices of possible feed substitutes, also influence the price of corn.

What is really interesting about seasonals is that although many traders know them and even use them, seasonals continue to exist. This is because there are enough traders that do not either use or believe in the correctness of seasonals. These traders often "fade" the market by going against the normal seasonal trends.

Life would be extremely simple for the futures trader if all he had to do was identify seasonals and place his trades accordingly. Unfortunately, neither life nor investing are ever that simple. There are trends (known as counter-seasonals) which, as you can tell by their name, act opposite to the normal seasonal tendencies.

These counter-seasonal trends can be explosive! While they do not happen with the regularity of normal seasonals, when they do happen they offer the opportunity for substantial profits. For example, in June of 1974 the December Corn market was trading in the $2.50 to $3.00 range. Around this time corn normally makes its seasonal highs, and then declines. In this instance, however, December corn rallied, making new seasonal highs well into the later part of the year, instead of dropping in price.

My *Mega-Seasonals Method* was designed not only to trade the normal seasonal cycle, but also to take advantage of the most favorable counter-seasonal trends. Some *Mega-Seasonals* trades are entered on either side of the market for this very reason. *Mega-Seasonals* has identified specific time periods when a market normally begins a mega-move. *Mega-Seasonals* lets the market dictate entry decisions.

The *Mega-Seasonals System* differs in many ways from other seasonal methods. The first being *Mega-Seasonals* is not just a buy or sell on a certain date type of system. *Mega-Seasonals* lets the market signal a seasonal or a counter-seasonal trend. *Mega Seasonals* does this by using a simple channel breakout entry overlaid with a specific time window (explained more completely in the next chapter). By using this entry format you will avoid many losing trades that other seasonal methods would take. An added advantage of this entry method is that it will give you more confidence in the trade, since the market is already moving in your direction and not against you as might be the case in a simple date entry system. "The trend is your friend" is one of the best and oldest maxims in the business of trading. By availing yourself of the *Mega-Seasonals Method* you will always be with "your friend" on the profitable side of the trend.

Another difference *Mega-Seasonals* offers over other seasonal methods is a higher profit to loss ratio. By using a market oriented protective stop instead of a fixed percentage or fixed dollar risk, *Mega-Seasonals* has limited the risk. My approach lets market volatility determine the risk and doesn't use just a "one size fits all" stop.

A third difference between more traditional seasonal methods and *Mega-Seasonals* is the use of trailing stops. Most other seasonal methods exit the market either through protective stops (at a loss) or on a specific date (at either a profit or loss). *Mega-Seasonals* uses a trailing stop, thereby protecting some of the profit your trade has earned. No one likes to see a profit deteriorate into a loss while waiting for the correct exit date. Some seasonal systems avoid this problem by taking a profit after a very short time. This has the effect of cutting down on total profits and decreasing the profit to loss ratio. But, of course, this is in direct opposition to another of the market maxims, "Cut your losses short and let your profits run." The *Mega-Seasonals Method* trades for longer time periods and for maximum profits per trade.

A fourth difference is that *Mega-Seasonals* uses only seasonal charts on futures to discover possible trades. Many other systems use cash seasonals charts. There are times that cash and futures seasonals differ greatly. I've included a seasonal futures chart for each of the *Mega-Seasonals* trades. This should help you visualize each trade more clearly and provide psychological support.

Finally, a fifth difference is that the *Mega-Seasonals Method* trades not only agricultural futures (as do others) but trades some very accurate and significantly profitable seasonal cycles in the financial markets. Many traders feel there are no seasonal tendencies in the financial markets. I believe otherwise.

For instance, the T-Bond market – and other interest rate markets – are very dependent on the Federal Government's borrowing, as well as the timing of income tax receipts. These are surely more forecastable than next week's or next month's weather. I'm sure we all know the date our Federal Income Tax Returns are due. We're constantly bombarded with countdowns on local and national television. When was the last time the television news mentioned the number of cattle on feed, or the size of the cocoa crop on the African Gold Coast?

For a moment let us replace the December Corn supply/demand rationale with that of the T-Bond market. Let me remind you that the cash T-Bond market is the primary way the federal government raises money to pay for its many programs. The 30-Year Treasury Bond is an extension of the cash market. An unusually large amount of federal funds are needed during the months of March and April when the federal government must refund overpaid income taxes, while continuing the funding of its other programs. This results in an urgent need for money. The federal government must raise these funds by increasing the Treasury Bonds available for sale. This increase in the supply of T-Bonds drives market prices lower during these months, just as the increase in corn supplies during harvest drives the price of corn lower. No matter what the commodity, greater supplies yield lower prices.

After March and April, the money starts pouring into government coffers from those of us who owe taxes. This creates a temporary surplus. Often then the federal government decreases the sale of T-Bonds, and T-Bond prices rally.

The following June T-Bond Seasonal Chart shows exactly what we've been discussing.

JUNE T-BONDS

1978-1997

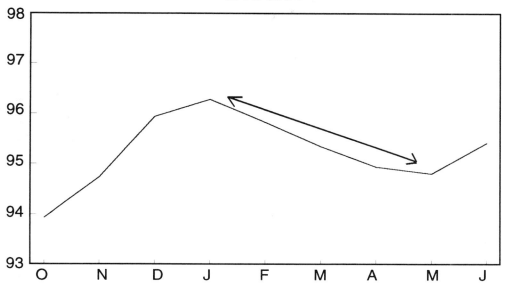

Just as our discussion of the December Corn market was boiled down to the simplest of terms, so here have I simplified the supply/demand factors in the T-Bond/Debt Instrument markets. Demand factors outside of the government, such as new housing starts, existing home sales, new automobile sales and a score of others also have an effect on these markets.

When choosing the 41 final "Ultra-Reliable" trades for this book, I had several overwhelming considerations and requirements that had to be met. Each trade must:

1. Have an excellent high percentage of both profitable trades and profitable years.

2. Have had very few inactive years.

3. Be supported by a solid and genuine fundamental rationale.

4. Use only the simplest entry and exit methods.

5. Post either a high profit-to-loss ratio or an impressive Profit Factor. (The Profit Factor is calculated by dividing the total profits by the total losses figure. This equates to the dollars won for every dollar lost.)

6. Have large dollar profits per trade.

7. Have a low dollar risk per trade relative to potential profits.

8. For the most part be an "undiscovered" seasonal, not one generally known or published elsewhere.

I believe that the 41 trades that make up my "Ultra-Reliable Seasonal Trades" all meet these requirements quite well. (Note: I've made a point to include a number of trades that utilize smaller size contracts so that any size trading account can participate.)

- Chapter 2 -

THE TECHNICAL TECHNIQUES AT THE HEART OF THE MEGA-SEASONALS METHOD

Mega-Seasonals uses only one entry/exit signal, the "channel breakout." The channel breakout is one of the simplest and most effective mechanical signals. The logic behind this signal is grounded in the market principle of buying a new high and selling a new low. It follows the old market maxim of "buying on strength and selling on weakness." The channel breakout employs no extensive mathematics, only very simple addition and subtraction. It's so simple, it can easily be performed by hand. In the following pages I will thoroughly explain each aspect of my method. Then I will walk you through two examples of actual historical Mega-Seasonal trades.

First, a few elementary definitions.

"What is a channel?"

A channel is a band of prices covering a specific time period. The top of the price band (or channel) is the highest price made during the time period. The bottom of the price band (or channel) is the lowest price made during the time period. Therefore, a four day price channel would be a band of prices with the top boundary being the highest price of the last four days and the bottom boundary being the lowest price of the last four days. *Mega-Seasonals* uses channels for entries, exits and protective stops. This allows the actual market volatility to determine important points in a market's price.

Let's construct a 4-day channel high from the following S&P data.

DATE	HIGH	4-DAY HIGH
12/08/92	438.60	
12/09/92	438.20	
12/10/92	436.20	
12/11/92	435.35	438.60

You can see that the highest price in this four day period is 438.60, made on 12/08/92. Now let's add a day.

DATE	HIGH	4-DAY HIGH
12/08/92	438.60	(this price is no longer within the 4-day time period)
12/09/92	438.20	
12/10/92	436.20	
12/11/92	435.35	438.60 (12/08 thru 12/11)
12/14/92	436.55	438.20 (12/09 thru 12/14)

Now the highest price in this new 4-day high channel is 438.20, made on 12/09/92. The 438.60, made on 12/08/92 is no longer within the 4-day channel time period. That's all there is to building a 4-day channel high. Of course, building a 4-day channel low uses the low prices of the last four days. All of the Mega-Seasonal entries and exits are built this way. If you are going to be doing this by hand, you should design a trade data sheet like the ones following each of the two example trades. If, on the other hand, you are computerized, most of the basic charting programs already have the channel breakout built-in.

"What is a breakout?"

A breakout, as employed in a channel breakout system, is the penetration of the price band by a specific number of points or ticks.

Two more simple, well-known concepts you will need to understand are "Protective Stops" and "Profit Stops." These are simple channel breakout techniques employed to exit positions.

The Protective Stop is the original stop used to protect you from unknown losses. Always compute this number each day your entry order is active/unfilled. You will be able to evaluate your risk and enter your Protective Stop when your fill is reported. This represents your approximate risk on a trade and should be watched for purposes of risk management.

The Profit Stop is a channel breakout that trails the market by a specific number of trading days. The Long Profit Stop is activated when the lowest price in the time period is greater than the entry price. Note: *this is the price that you used to enter the market, not the price at which you are filled.*

Now that you have a clearer picture of the channel breakout, let's look at our first example: The Mega-Seasonals S&P 500 Index Trade #3. The rules (and explanations) for this trade are as follows:

Rules for S&P 500 Index Trade #3:

1. Enters long March S&P from December 15th through January 17th. (This is the trade entry window for this trade. Only during this time period do you place entry orders.)

2. Place a long entry stop order 1 tick (the minimum price change) above the highest price of the last 4 trading days. (Add 1 tick to the highest price made during the previous 4 trading days. This is today's entry price. When the 4-day high drops, add 1 tick to the new 4-day high for your new entry stop. Continue this until your entry stop is filled or you are no longer in the trade entry window.)

3. When your order is filled, place a Protective Sell Stop 1 tick below the low of the last 5 trading days. (Find the lowest price made during the last 5 trading days, not counting the day of entry. Subtract 1 tick from that price. This is your protective stop for this trade. This Protective Sell Stop price will not change until the Profit Stop is greater than the entry price.)

4. When the low of the last 5 trading days is equal to or greater than the entry price, raise your stop to 1 tick below the lowest price of the last 5 trading days. Keep raising this price as the lowest 5-day price increases. (Should you be stopped out by this Profit Stop and you are still in the trade entry window time period, immediately – the same time your fill is reported – begin placing entry orders again as in #2.)

5. There is no Date Exit for this trade. Continue entering the Profit Stop as explained in #4 until stopped out. Should you not get stopped out and the March S&P goes off the board, don't worry. The S&P contract is settled in cash. Your trade will automatically be closed at the very last price. (Most Mega-Seasonal trades have a Date Exit. The rules for each trade will fully explain the procedure for exiting.)

Now let's walk through a "Trade Action Diary" of the 1993 Mega-Seasonals S&P Trade #3. Following this diary is the March 1993 S&P daily trade data used in this diary and a chart to aid you in visualization. Please refer to these as needed. (At the time of this trade, the minimum fluctuation of the S&P contract

– i.e. minimum tick – was 5 points and the contract valuation was $500 times the index. These have since changed to a minimum tick of 10 points and a contract valuation of $250 times the index.)

DATE	**NOTATIONS**
12/15/92 (pre-open)	This is the first day to enter the Mega-Seasonals S&P Index Trade #3. Referring to the daily trade data, you can see that the highest price in the previous 4 trading days is 438.20, made on 12/09/92. (This data is the same data we used to explain how to build a 4-day high channel.) Call your broker and enter an order to buy 1 March 93 S&P at 438.25 (438.20 plus 5 points) stop, good until cancelled.
12/16/92 (pre-open)	The 4 -day high has dropped to 436.55, made on 12/14/92. Call your broker and cancel and replace your entry order at the new price of 436.60 (436.55 plus 5 points).
12/17/92	Your broker calls with your fill. You bought 1 March S&P at 436.60. (See chart on page 18.) Now you must enter a protective stop for this trade. As I've said, it is always best to compute the protective stop each day your entry order is active. Rule #3 states that your protective stop should be 1 tick (5 points) below the lowest price of the last 5 trading days. Looking at the daily trade data, you see that the low is 431.40, made on 12/16/92. The protective stop for this trade is 431.35 (431.40 less 5 points). There is one more thing to do before you enter this stop. Ask your broker what today's low has been. If today's low is above the protective stop of 431.35, then 431.35 is the protective stop. If, on the other hand, today's low had been less than 431.35, subtract 5 points from today's low. This is the protective stop. (This rarely happens, but always check the low – or high if entering short – with your broker.)

12/24/92

(pre-open)   The 5-day low has moved up to 432.20, made on 12/17/92. You are watching this number, waiting for it to be equal to or greater than your entry price of 436.60. This 432.20 is still less than your entry, so no action is taken. You continue tracking this number as it increases.

12/28/92

(pre-open)   The 5-day low is 437.60, made on 12/18/92. This number is greater than your entry price of 436.60. Call your broker and cancel, and replace your protective stop with the new Profit Stop price of 437.55 (437.60 less 5 points).

12/30/92   Your broker calls with your fill on the Profit Stop. You sold 1 March 92 S&P at 437.55 for a gross profit of $475. (See chart on page 18.) Since we are still in the trade window time period for this trade, you enter a new long entry stop at 443.85, good until cancelled. This price is the 4-day high of 443.80, made on 12/29/92 plus 1 tick or 5 points.

01/06/93

(pre-open)   The high of 443.80 is no longer in the 4-day time period. The new 4-day high is 440.35, made on 12/31/92. Call your broker, cancel and replace your entry price to 440.40 (440.35 plus 5 points).

01/08/93

(pre-open)   There is a new 4-day high of 438.65, made on 01/04/93. Call your broker and lower your entry stop to 438.70.

01/11/93

(pre-open)   The high of 438.65 has been replaced by the high of 436.50, made on 01/07/93. Call your broker and lower your entry stop to 436.55.

01/14/93 (pre-open)	The high of 436.50 is no longer within the 4-day channel. The new 4-day high is 434.15, made on 01/13/93. Call your broker and lower your entry stop to 434.20, good until cancelled.
01/14/93	Your broker calls with your fill. You bought 1 March 93 S&P contract at 434.20. (See chart on page 18.) You checked the trade data this morning and saw that the lowest price for the previous 5 trading days is 426.70, made on 01/08/93. The Protective Stop for this trade is 426.65, unless today's low has been less. You ask your broker for today's low and find out it is above 426.65. You enter a protective stop of 426.65, good until cancelled. Now you wait for the Profit Stop to be activated.
01/29/93 (pre-open)	You've been watching the 5-day low rise and it is now at 435.20, made on 01/22/93. This is greater than your entry price of 434.20. Call your broker and cancel your protective stop and replace it with a stop at 435.15.
02/01/93 (pre-open)	The 5-day low has risen to 436.10. Call your broker and raise your stop to 436.05, good until cancelled.
02/02/93 (pre-open)	Again the 5-day low has risen. The new 5-day low is 436.60. This raises your Profit Stop to 436.55. Call your broker and raise your stop to 436.55. (These rapidly rising stops are just what we want to lock in greater and greater profits.)
02/04/93 (pre-open)	The 5-day low has increased again. Call your broker with the new stop price of 436.75.
02/08/93 (pre-open)	The 5-day low of 436.80 is no longer in the 5-day time period. The new 5-day low is 439.00, made on 02/01/93. Call your broker and change the Profit Stop to 438.95.

02/09/93
(pre-open)   Again the 5-day low has moved higher. Call your broker, cancel and replace your stop price to 440.85.

02/10/93
(pre-open)   Another new 5-day low of 443.15, made on 02/03/93. Call your broker and raise your stop to 443.10.

02/12/93
(pre-open)   The 5-day low has risen to 444.25. Call your broker and raise your profit stop to 444.20, good until cancelled.

02/16/93   Your broker calls with your fill. You sold your March 93 S&P contract at 443.70 for a profit of $4,750. (See chart on page 18.) Since you are no longer in the trade window time period, this trade is over for this year. Pocket your profits and wait for this trade next year.

MARCH 93 S&P INDEX

DATE	HIGH	LOW	4-DAY HIGH	5-DAY LOW
12/08/92	438.60	435.25		
	438.20	434.25		
	436.20	433.30		
	435.35	433.85	438.60	
12/14/92	436.55	433.35	438.20	433.30
	435.10	433.10	436.55	433.10
	435.30	431.40	436.55	431.40
	436.85	432.20	436.85	431.40
	442.00	437.60	442.00	431.40
12/21/92	442.55	440.60	442.55	431.40
	442.90	439.35	442.90	431.40
	442.60	440.10	442.90	432.20
	441.30	440.40	442.90	437.60
12/28/92	440.50	437.60	442.90	437.60
	443.80	437.60	443.80	437.60
	440.10	437.10	443.80	437.10
	440.35	436.65	443.80	436.65
01/04/93	438.65	434.70	443.80	434.70
	436.20	433.70	440.35	433.70
	436.10	432.90	440.35	432.90
	436.50	429.50	438.65	429.50
	430.75	426.70	436.50	426.70
01/11/93	431.65	429.10	436.50	426.70
	431.80	427.90	436.50	426.70
	434.15	430.15	434.15	426.70
	436.70	432.90	436.70	426.70
	440.20	435.90	440.20	427.90
01/18/93	437.50	435.65	440.20	427.90
	438.15	434.80	440.20	430.15
	436.80	432.75	440.20	432.75
	436.50	432.30	438.15	432.30
	438.10	435.20	438.15	432.30

MARCH 93 S&P INDEX

DATE	HIGH	LOW	4-DAY HIGH	5-DAY LOW
01/25/93	440.80	436.10	440.80	432.30
	443.05	439.15	443.05	432.30
	440.20	436.60	443.05	432.30
	439.45	437.00	443.05	435.20
	439.70	436.80	443.05	436.10
02/01/93	442.65	439.00	442.65	436.60
	443.30	440.90	443.30	436.60
	448.00	443.15	448.00	436.80
	450.50	448.10	450.50	436.80
	450.25	447.05	450.50	439.00
02/08/93	450.85	447.90	450.85	440.90
	447.65	445.05	450.85	443.15
	447.25	444.25	450.85	444.25
	450.20	447.30	450.85	444.25
	448.05	444.60	450.20	444.25
02/16/93	444.10	432.80	450.20	432.80
	434.70	431.65	450.20	431.65

18

March 93 S & P

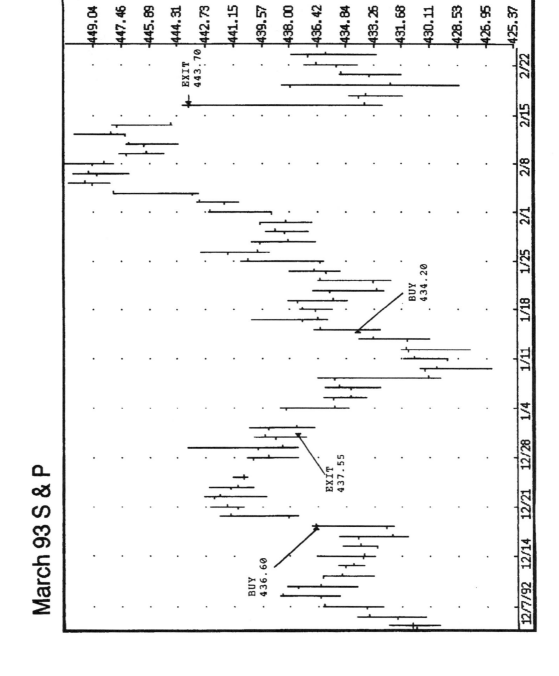

Now, let's look at a slightly more complicated Mega-Seasonals trade, the Japanese Yen Trade #1. The only difference being, this trade enters on either side of the market. This is Mega-Seasonals most complicated entry. In the interest of simplicity this entry is used infrequently. It may be helpful to think of the long entry and the short entry as two separate trades. Each trade is the same as the one we just walked through, but using a different channel size. You will need to enter both long and short orders with your broker during the trade entry window. The rules for this trade are:

Rules for Japanese Yen Trade #1:

1. Enters long and short June Yen from the 2nd trading day of February through March 21st. (This is the trade entry window for this trade.)

2. Place a long entry stop 7 ticks above the high of the last 22 trading days and place a short entry stop 7 ticks below the low of the last 22 trading days. (When either the 22 day high or the 22 day low changes, you must recalculate the new entry price by adding or subtracting 7 points. Then call your broker and replace the existing order.)

3. When filled:
   On long: Place a Protective Sell Stop 1 tick below the low of the last six trading days.

   On short: Place a Protective Buy Stop 1 tick above the high of the last six trading days.

   Remember to continue entering the opposite entry order as described in #2, until you are no longer in the trade entry window. Should you already have entered a trade via #2 and the reverse entry price is greater than either your protective sell stop or profit stop (for longs) use the entry price to exit the current trade so that your new position is short. Of course, should you presently be short, adjust the protective buy stop or profit stop.

4. If long: When the low of the last 22 trading days is equal to or greater than the long entry price, raise your stop to 1 tick below the low of the last 22 trading days. (If you are stopped out by this

Profit Stop and you are still in the trade entry window, begin placing long entry orders again as outlined in #2.)

If short: When the high of the last 22 trading days is equal to or less than the short entry price, lower your stop to 1 tick above the 22 day high. (If you are stopped out by this Profit Stop while still in the trade entry window, begin entering short entry orders again as outlined in #2.)

5. Exit this trade on the close of the first trading day after April 14th. (This is the Date Exit mentioned earlier. It is self-explanatory, as are those of other Mega-Seasonals trades.)

Now let's walk through a "Trade Action Diary" of the 1995 Mega-Seasonals Japanese Yen Trade #1. If the rules above were somewhat confusing, this will help you to more thoroughly understand this method. Following the Trade Action Diary is the June 1995 Yen daily trade data used in this diary, and a chart to help you visualize the trade. Please refer to them as needed.

DATE

NOTATIONS

02/02/95
(pre-open)   This is the first day to enter the Japanese Yen Trade #1. Referring to the daily trade data (beginning on page 25), you can see that the highest price in the last 22 trading days is 1.0380, made on 01/16/95 and that the lowest price in the last 22 trading days is 1.0052. Before you place your entry stops you must add 7 ticks (or points) to the 22 day high. The long entry price is 1.0387 (1.0380 plus 7). The short entry price is 1.0045 (1.0052 less 7 points). Call your broker and place both of these entry stops good until cancelled. (Note: should a new high be made that is less than the 7 points you added to the old 22 day high, you will not be filled. Tomorrow, you would add 7 points to this new high and enter a new price with your broker. Should a new low be made that does not hit your short price, subtract 7 points from this new low for your new short entry price.)

02/08/95

(pre-open)   The new 22 day low has risen to 1.0099. Call your broker and cancel and replace your short entry stop price to 1.0092 (1.0099 less 7 points).

02/09/95

(pre-open)   The 22 day low of yesterday (1.0099) is no longer within the 22 day period. The new 22 day low is 1.0148. Call your broker and cancel and replace your short sale order price to 1.0141 (1.0148 made on 01/10/95, less 7 points).

02/10/95

(pre-open)   The 22 day low has risen to 1.0154. Call your broker and cancel and replace your short entry price to 1.0147.

02/16/95

(pre-open)   Not to be outdone, the 22 day high has now fallen to 1.0343, made on 01/30/95. The price channel is narrowing. Call your broker and move your long entry stop to 1.0350 (1.0343 plus 7 points).

02/16/95   Your broker calls with a fill on the long entry stop. You bought 1 June Yen at the gap opening of 1.0360. (See chart on page 28.) Now, you must enter a protective stop for this long trade. The rules say that your stop should be 1 tick under the 6 day low. Looking at the daily data, you can see that the 6 day low is 1.0213, made on 02/10/95. The Protective Stop for this trade is 1.0212. But check with your broker for today's low. The low is above the 1.0212 protective stop, so you enter a Protective Sell Stop at 1.0212. Do **not** cancel your short <u>entry</u> order. The sell order you just entered is meant to protect your new long position. The lower priced short is in place to get you short 1 contract.

02/24/25

(pre-open)   There is a new 22 day low of 1.0160. Call your broker and move your short entry stop to 1.0153.

03/09/95

(pre-open)   The low of 1.0160 is out of the 22 day channel time frame. The new 22 day low is 1.0186. Call your broker and cancel and replace your short entry stop price to 1.0179.

03/10/95

(pre-open)   The 22 day low has risen again. Call your broker and change your short entry stop price to 1.0194 (the 22 day low of 1.0201, made on 02/07/95, less 7 ticks).

03/13/95

(pre-open)   There is another new 22 day low at 1.0213. Call your broker and change your short entry price to 1.0206.

03/16/95

(pre-open)   The low of 1.0213 is out of the 22 day range. The low of 1.0240 is now the 22 day low. Call your broker and change both your short entry price order and protective stop order to 1.0233. (Entry orders take precedence and replace any protective stop and profit stop orders!)

03/20/95

(pre-open)   A new 22 day low of 1.0281 is now active. Call your broker and cancel, changing <u>both</u> your short order prices to 1.0274.

03/21/95

(pre-open)   The 1.0281 low is no longer within the 22 day time period. The new low is 1.0360. Referring to #4 in the trade rules you can see that the 22 day low is also the Profit Stop channel low. Since this price is equal to your entry price (remember, not the fill price), you raise the stop on your long trade. The new price for this stop will be 1.0359 (1.0360 less 1 tick). Call your broker and change the short <u>entry</u> price to 1.0353 (1.0360 less 7 points).

03/22/95

(pre-open)   Call your broker and cancel your short <u>entry</u> stop of 1.0353. You are no longer in the trade entry time period, so a short trade should no longer be entered. Also, there is a new low of 1.0373, made on 02/17/95. Raise your Profit Stop price to 1.0372.

03/23/95
(pre-open)   The 22 day low of 1.0373 has slightly increased to 1.0374. Call your broker and raise your Profit Stop price to 1.0373. (The 1.0374 less 1 tick.)

03/30/95
(pre-open)   A new 22 day low of 1.0411 has replaced the old 22 day low. The higher and the faster the market moves your way, the more often you will need to move your stop. Call your broker, cancel and replace your stop price to 1.0410.

03/31/95
(pre-open)   Another new low, call your broker and raise your stop price to 1.0430.

04/04/95
(pre-open)   A big jump in the 22 low, call your broker and raise your profit stop price to 1.0579.

04/05/95
(pre-open)   Another big jump in the 22 day low. Call your broker, change the price on your sell stop to 1.0764 (1.0765 less 1 point).

04/06/95
(pre-open)   This market has really moved. Call your broker and increase your stop price to 1.0879.

04/07/95
(pre-open)   Just continue to raise this stop. The higher it is, the more profit you are protecting. Call your broker and change your sell price to 1.0939.

04/11/95
(pre-open)   Call your broker and change the Profit Stop price to 1.0999 (1.1000 less 1 point).

24

04/12/95

(pre-open)   You again call your broker (who by now has changed your trade card a few times) and tell him to raise your Profit Stop price to 1.1051.

04/17/95

(pre-open)   Call your broker, cancel and replace your price on the sell stop to 1.124. Since this is the date exit for this trade, enter an order to "sell 1 June Yen Close Only."

04/18/95   Your broker calls you for a change. You sold your June 95 Yen contract at 1.2288, for a profit of $24,100. (See chart on page 28.) Pretty good pay for a few minutes of record keeping and a couple of dozen phone calls. Remember to cancel your Profit Stop.

If this has been somewhat confusing, I can tell you from experience that it sounds more complicated than it is. Besides which, over $24,000 in profits for slightly more than two months work is not bad pay! Wonder what that works out to on a per hour basis?

MARCH 95 JAPANESE YEN

DATE	HIGH	LOW	22-DAY HIGH	22-DAY LOW
01/03/95	1.0187	1.0140		
	1.0105	1.0052		
	1.0108	1.0088		
	1.0105	1.0052		
01/09/95	1.0230	1.0099		
	1.0185	1.0148		
	1.0209	1.0179		
	1.0320	1.0216		
	1.0340	1.0275		
01/16/95	1.0380	1.0324		
	1.0308	1.0262		
	1.0269	1.0202		
	1.0310	1.0175		
	1.0265	1.0216		
01/23/95	1.0230	1.0154		
	1.0256	1.0197		
	1.0250	1.0196		
	1.0244	1.0222		
	1.0262	1.0205		
01/30/95	1.0343	1.0268		
	1.0310	1.0185		
02/01/95	1.0240	1.0200	1.0380	1.0052
	1.0220	1.0188	1.0380	1.0052
	1.0222	1.0160	1.0380	1.0052
02/06/95	1.0237	1.0186	1.0380	1.0052
	1.0231	1.0201	1.0380	1.0099
	1.0275	1.0252	1.0380	1.0148
	1.0267	1.0244	1.0380	1.0154
	1.0272	1.0213	1.0380	1.0154
02/13/95	1.0295	1.0270	1.0380	1.0154
	1.0300	1.0240	1.0380	1.0154
	1.0322	1.0281	1.0343	1.0154
	1.0411	1.0360	1.0411	1.0154
	1.0442	1.0373	1.0442	1.0154

MARCH 95 JAPANESE YEN

DATE	HIGH	LOW	22-DAY HIGH	22-DAY LOW
02/21/95	1.0434	1.0393	1.0442	1.0154
	1.0464	1.0400	1.0464	1.0154
	1.0472	1.0420	1.0472	1.0160
	1.0490	1.0395	1.0490	1.0160
02/27/95	1.0480	1.0374	1.0490	1.0160
	1.0486	1.0411	1.0490	1.0160
03/01/95	1.0490	1.0454	1.0490	1.0160
	1.0650	1.0431	1.0650	1.0160
	1.0798	1.0580	1.0798	1.0160
03/06/95	1.0950	1.0765	1.0950	1.0160
	1.1325	1.0880	1.1325	1.0160
	1.1390	1.1010	1.1390	1.0186
	1.1215	1.0940	1.1390	1.0201
	1.1183	1.1000	1.1390	1.0213
03/13/95	1.1253	1.1102	1.1390	1.0213
	1.1160	1.1052	1.1390	1.0213
	1.1317	1.1125	1.1390	1.0240
	1.1340	1.1183	1.1390	1.0240
	1.1370	1.1186	1.1390	1.0281
03/20/95	1.1390	1.1240	1.1390	1.0360
	1.1440	1.1290	1.1440	1.0373
	1.1394	1.1300	1.1440	1.0374
	1.1480	1.1340	1.1480	1.0374
	1.1457	1.1305	1.1480	1.0374
03/27/95	1.1397	1.1249	1.1480	1.0374
	1.1395	1.1248	1.1480	1.0374
	1.1470	1.1330	1.1480	1.0411
	1.1452	1.1209	1.1480	1.0431
	1.1697	1.1240	1.1697	1.0431
04/03/95	1.1740	1.1580	1.1740	1.0580
	1.1789	1.1649	1.1789	1.0765
	1.1775	1.1652	1.1789	1.0880
	1.1855	1.1690	1.1855	1.0940
	1.2055	1.1815	1.2055	1.0940

MARCH 95 JAPANESE YEN

DATE	HIGH	LOW	22-DAY HIGH	22-DAY LOW
04/10/95	1.2446	1.1950	1.2446	1.1000
	1.2100	1.1903	1.2446	1.1052
	1.2130	1.1950	1.2446	1.1052
	1.2155	1.2023	1.2446	1.1125
04/17/95	1.2350	1.2146	1.2446	1.1183

June 95 Yen

BUY
1.0360

EXIT
1.2288

125.49
123.80
122.12
120.44
118.75
117.07
115.39
113.70
112.02
110.34
108.65
106.97
105.29
103.60
101.92
100.24

1/23/95 1/30 2/6 2/13 2/20 2/27 3/6 3/13 3/20 3/27 4/3 4/10 4/17 4/2

- Chapter 3 -

30 YEAR TREASURY BOND

The Chicago Board of Trade began trading futures contracts on the 30 Year U. S. Treasury Bond in 1977. Options on these futures started trading in 1982. The face value of the Board of Trade contract is $100,000. The MidAmerica Commodity Exchange trades a half-sized $50,000 contract. U. S. Treasury Bonds are 30 year debt instruments the Federal Government sells to finance its operations.

Since the U. S. Government is the seller of Treasury Bonds, they control the supply coming to market. From January to May the federal government must sell large amounts of T-Bonds to not only finance present spending but to pay tax refunds. These sales decrease in May as the government is flooded with income tax payments.

On the demand side of the pricing equation are the numerous types of investors bidding for the bonds. There is a seasonality to their demand also. During the first months of the new year some of these investors find they must partially sell their holdings to finance income tax payments. This selling weighs on the T-Bond market, causing a decline.

The price of the 30 Year Treasury Bond is affected by many reports issued by the government and private institutions. Some of the reports to keep an eye on are New Home Sales, Existing Home Sales, Employment and Unemployment Statistics, GDP and Producer and Consumer Price Indices, as well as the results from FOMC meetings.

30 YEAR US TREASURY BOND TRADE #1

There is almost an unbelievable downward trend in the June T-Bond contract starting in the January/February time frame. This is the time when the federal government most needs funds, thereby increasing the volume of bond sales. Also, investors often need to sell bonds to raise cash to pay income tax liabilities. This causes a glut on all government debt instrument markets, driving prices lower. Every so often this trade turns "counter-seasonal" and begins a long-term rally. *Mega-Seasonals* trades both sides of this market, profiting from the move that develops. The June T-Bond Seasonal Chart shows the decline quite well. Mega-Seasonals T-Bond Trade #1 has been profitable 85% of the 20 years it has traded, accruing a profit of $77,437.

PERFORMANCE HISTORY (1978-1997)

Total Profit $77,437
Total Years Examined 20
Profit Years 17 (85%)
Loss Years 3 (15%)
Inactive Years 0
Average Profit $5,037
Average Loss $2,729
Profit-to-Loss Ratio 1.8
Total Profits/Total Losses 10.5

JUNE T-BONDS

1978-1997

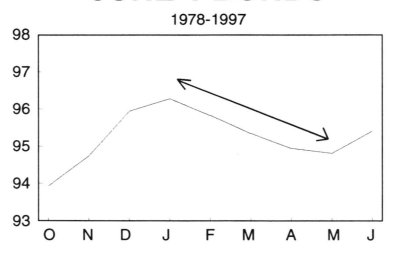

Rules for T-Bond Trade #1:

1. Enters long and short June T-Bonds from the first trading day after January 9th through the last trading day of February.

2. Place a long entry stop 10 ticks above the 12 day high. Place a short entry stop 10 ticks under the 12 day low. Changing these entries as necessary.

3. When filled:
   On long: Place a protective sell stop 1 point below the 5 day low.
   On short: Place a protective buy stop 1 point above the 5 day high.

   Remember to continue entering the opposite entry as described in #2 above, until you are no longer in the trade entry window. (Should you already have entered a trade via #2 and the reverse entry price is greater than either your protective sell stop or profit stop (for longs), use the entry price to exit the current trade so that your new position is short. Of course, should you presently be short, you adjust the protective buy stop or profit stop.)

4. If long: When the low of the last 21 trading days is equal to or greater than the entry price, raise your stop to 1 tick below the 21 day low.

   If short: When the high of the last 21 trading days is equal to or less than the entry price, lower your stop to 1 tick above the 21 day high.

5. Exit this trade on the close of the first trading day after May 5th.

Historical Results for T-Bond Trade #1
June T-Bonds

USM	ENTRY DATE	L/S	PRICE	EXIT DATE	EXIT METHOD	PRICE	TRADE P/L	YEARLY P/L
1978	01/11/78	S	96 22	05/08/78	DATEX	95 00	$ 1,688	$ 1,688
1979	01/25/79	L	91 27	02/07/79	REV	90 09	$ (1,563)	
	02/07/79	S	90 09	05/07/79	DATEX	87 26	$ 2,469	$ 906
1980	01/17/80	S	79 25	03/18/80	PSTOP	70 19	$ 9,188	$ 9,188
1981	01/21/81	S	70 02	03/13/81	PSTOP	68 21	$ 1,406	$ 1,406
1982	01/26/82	L	60 14	02/04/82	PROTS	58 15	$ (1,969)	
	02/08/82	S	58 00	02/18/82	PROTS	60 01	$ (2,031)	
	02/18/82	L	60 10	03/29/82	PSTOP	61 07	$ 906	$ (3,094)
1983	01/19/83	S	75 10	02/11/83	REV	74 06	$ 1,125	
	02/11/83	L	74 06	05/06/83	DATEX	79 19	$ 5,406	$ 6,531
1984	01/13/84	L	70 17	02/13/84	PROTS	69 10	$ (1,219)	
	02/13/84	S	69 04	05/07/84	DATEX	63 07	$ 5,906	$ 4,687
1985	01/23/85	L	71 22	02/20/85	REV	70 05	$ (1,531)	
	02/20/85	S	70 05	03/29/85	PSTOP	69 11	$ 813	$ (718)
1986	01/13/86	S	81 08	01/28/86	REV	83 30	$ (2,688)	
	01/28/86	L	83 30	05/06/86	DATEX	100 16	$ 16,563	$ 13,875
1987	01/26/87	S	98 19	02/24/87	REV	100 07	$ (1,625)	
	02/24/87	L	100 07	03/31/87	PROTS	97 15	$ (2,750)	$ (4,375)
1988	01/15/88	L	89 00	03/17/88	PSTOP	91 13	$ 2,406	$ 2,406
1989	01/13/89	L	89 30	02/09/89	REV	89 27	$ (94)	
	02/09/89	S	89 27	04/03/89	PSTOP	88 29	$ 938	$ 844
1990	01/12/90	S	96 29	05/07/90	DATEX	90 13	$ 6,500	$ 6,500
1991	02/01/91	L	96 24	02/22/91	REV	96 14	$ (313)	
	02/22/91	S	96 14	04/04/91	PSTOP	95 26	$ 625	$ 312
1992	01/14/92	S	101 27	04/03/92	PSTOP	99 21	$ 2,188	$ 2,188
1993	01/19/93	L	104 22	03/29/93	PSTOP	108 22	$ 4,000	$ 4,000
1994	01/12/94	L	115 26	02/04/94	REV	114 00	$ (1,813)	
	02/04/94	S	114 00	05/06/94	DATEX	102 15	$ 11,531	$ 9,718
1995	01/27/95	L	100 15	05/08/95	DATEX	108 30	$ 8,469	$ 8,469
1996	02/16/96	S	117 32	05/06/96	DATEX	107 05	$ 10,844	$ 10,844
1997	02/03/97	L	111 20	02/26/97	REV	111 01	$ (594)	
	02/26/97	S	111 01	04/29/97	PSTOP	108 12	$ 2,656	$ 2,062

TOTAL $ 77,437

Exit Legend:

DATEX = Exit Date
PROTS = Protective Stop
PSTOP = Profit Stop
REV   = Reverse Entry

30 YEAR US TREASURY BOND TRADE #2

As you can see from the September T-Bond Seasonal Chart, there is an extremely powerful upward trend beginning in May and topping out in July. I believe this to partially be the result of an increase in investable income from tax refunds; and in part to lower marketings of T-Bonds by the federal government because of a temporary surplus of funds received from tax payments. Thus, we have increased demand and decreased supply of T-Bonds. A perfect supply/demand picture for a rally. Mega-Seasonals T-Bond Trade #2 has been profitable 13 of the last 16 years traded with a profit of $43,779.

PERFORMANCE HISTORY (1978-1997)

Total Profit	$43,779	
Total Years Examined	20	
Profit Years	13	(81%)
Loss Years	3	(19%)
Inactive Years	4	
Average Profit	$3,675	
Average Loss	$1,334	
Profit-to-Loss Ratio	2.8	
Total Profits/Total Losses	11.9	

SEPTEMBER T-BONDS

1978-1997

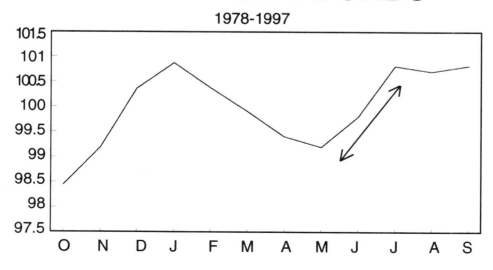

Rules for T-Bond Trade #2:

1. Enters long September T-Bonds from the first trading day of May through June 4th.

2. Place a long entry stop 6 ticks above the high of the last 12 trading days. Changing this price as needed.

3. When filled, place a protective sell stop 1 tick below the low of the last 4 trading days.

4. When the low of the last 12 trading days is equal to or greater than the entry price, move your stop up to 1 tick under the 12 day low. Keep raising this stop as necessary.

5. Exit this trade on the close of the first trading day after June 13th.

Historical Results for T-Bond Trade #2
September T-Bonds

USU	ENTRY DATE	L/S	PRICE	EXIT DATE	EXIT METHOD	PRICE		TRADE P/L		YEARLY P/L
1978	N/T						$	N/T	$	N/T
1979	05/17/79	L	88 30	06/14/79	DATEX	91 18	$	2,625	$	2,625
1980	05/01/80	L	79 00	06/16/80	DATEX	86 00	$	7,000	$	7,000
1981	05/18/81	L	64 14	06/15/81	DATEX	68 03	$	3,656	$	3,656
1982	N/T						$	N/T	$	N/T
1983	05/04/83	L	78 29	05/16/83	PROTS	77 17	$	(1,375)	$	(1,375)
1984	N/T						$	N/T	$	N/T
1985	05/10/85	L	71 24	06/14/85	DATEX	78 09	$	6,531	$	6,531
1986	N/T						$	N/T	$	N/T
1987	05/29/87	L	91 07	06/15/87	DATEX	92 20	$	1,406	$	1,406
1988	06/03/88	L	87 06	06/14/88	DATEX	89 18	$	2,375	$	2,375
1989	05/12/89	L	90 19	06/14/89	DATEX	96 16	$	5,906	$	5,906
1990	05/11/90	L	90 27	06/14/90	DATEX	94 23	$	3,875	$	3,875
1991	05/30/91	L	95 12	06/03/91	PROTS	94 06	$	(1,188)	$	(1,188)
1992	05/08/92	L	98 12	06/15/92	DATEX	99 24	$	1,375	$	1,375
1993	06/01/93	L	110 19	06/14/93	DATEX	111 27	$	1,250	$	1,250
1994	05/17/94	L	104 05	06/14/94	DATEX	104 22	$	531	$	531
1995	05/03/95	L	105 14	06/14/95	DATEX	114 03	$	8,656	$	8,656
1996	05/20/96	L	109 16	05/30/96	PROTS	108 02	$	(1,438)	$	(1,438)
1997	05/02/97	L	109 15	06/16/97	DATEX	112 02	$	2,594	$	2,594

TOTAL $ 43,779

Exit Legend:

DATEX = Exit Date
PROTS = Protective Stop
PSTOP = Profit Stop
REV   = Reverse Entry

30 YEAR US TREASURY BOND TRADE #3

The T-Bond trade #3 completes the year of T-Bond seasonals. It profits from the seasonal uptrend beginning in September and ending in mid-December. Money is pouring into investment funds during the latter quarter of the year to fund tax deferred 401K's and IRA's. The federal government is flush with extra cash from third quarter income tax quarterly payments. These fundamentals fuel the T-Bond rally, as you can see from the December T-Bond Seasonal Chart. Mega-Seasonals T-Bond Trade #3 has been profitable 76% of the years traded, earning a profit of $45,220.

PERFORMANCE HISTORY (1978-1997)

Total Profit...$45,220
Total Years Examined 20
Profit Years 13 (76%)
Loss Years 4 (24%)
Inactive Years 3
Average Profit...$4,099
Average Loss $2,016
Profit-to-Loss Ratio 2.0
Total Profits/Total Losses........................... 6.6

DECEMBER T-BONDS
1978-1997

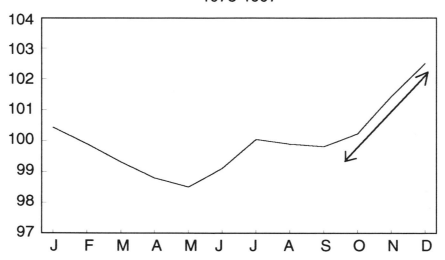

Rules for T-Bond Trade #3:

1. Enters long December T-Bonds from the first trading day of September through November 16th.

2. Place a long entry stop 5 ticks above the 24 day high.

3. When filled, place a protective sell stop 1 tick under the low of the last 5 trading days.

4. When the low of the last 22 trading days is equal to or greater than the entry price, move your stop up to 1 tick below the 22 day low. Move this stop as needed.

5. Exit this trade on the close of the first trading day after December 9th.

Historical Results for T-Bond Trade #3
December T-Bonds

USZ	ENTRY DATE	L/S	PRICE	EXIT DATE	EXIT METHOD	PRICE	TRADE P/L	YEARLY P/L
1978	09/08/78	L	96 03	09/20/78	PROTS	94 24	$ (1,344)	$ (1,344)
1979	N/T						$ N/T	$ N/T
1980	N/T						$ N/T	$ N/T
1981	11/05/81	L	60 29	12/10/81	DATEX	62 03	$ 1,188	$ 1,188
1982	09/21/82	L	69 19	12/10/82	DATEX	75 14	$ 5,844	$ 5,844
1983	09/12/83	L	72 16	12/12/83	DATEX	70 09	$ (2,219)	$ (2,219)
1984	09/10/84	L	66 14	12/10/84	DATEX	71 13	$ 4,969	$ 4,969
1985	10/17/85	L	76 13	12/10/85	DATEX	83 10	$ 6,906	$ 6,906
1986	10/30/86	L	98 10	12/10/86	DATEX	100 30	$ 2,625	$ 2,625
1987	10/22/87	L	84 00	12/08/87	PSTOP	86 14	$ 2,438	$ 2,438
1988	09/02/88	L	87 13	11/14/88	PSTOP	88 15	$ 1,063	$ 1,063
1989	10/06/89	L	98 01	12/11/89	DATEX	99 14	$ 1,406	$ 1,406
1990	10/01/90	L	89 27	12/10/90	DATEX	97 13	$ 7,563	$ 7,563
1991	09/12/91	L	98 13	12/10/91	DATEX	101 18	$ 3,156	$ 3,156
1992	09/04/92	L	106 04	10/09/92	PROTS	103 21	$ (2,469)	$ (2,469)
1993	09/02/93	L	118 27	11/02/93	PROTS	116 26	$ (2,031)	$ (2,031)
1994	N/T						$ N/T	$ N/T
1995	09/01/95	L	113 06	12/11/95	DATEX	120 18	$ 7,375	$ 7,375
1996	10/02/96	L	110 15	12/10/96	DATEX	114 23	$ 4,250	$ 4,250
1997	09/16/97	L	114 06	12/10/97	DATEX	118 22	$ 4,500	$ 4,500

TOTAL $ 45,220

Exit Legend:

DATEX = Exit Date
PROTS = Protective Stop
PSTOP = Profit Stop
REV   = Reverse Entry

- Chapter 4 -

LIVE CATTLE

Live Cattle futures (40,000 lbs.) began trading on the Chicago Mercantile Exchange in 1964. It was the first "live" product traded. In 1984 options on Live Cattle futures began trading. The MidAmerica Commodity Exchange trades a half sized contract of 20,000 lbs. The United States produces more cattle than any other country. The production of beef employs more land and creates more market value than does any other livestock.

The demand side of the cattle market is dominated by the relatively few large packers. Demand is not as volatile as supply. The relative price of substitute foods such as pork and poultry aid in price discovery.

The supply side of the pricing equation is dependent on the size of the calf crop, reported cattle inventories and slaughter weights. Extremes in weather conditions can also be a major price determinant. Take for instance a drought in the feed growing areas. This would increase the cost of feed, thereby compelling feeder operations to market their cattle earlier and at a lower weight than normal. This would depress the price in the cattle market and would most likely begin the normal multi-year cattle cycle.

There are three extremely important reports to watch when trading cattle: The Monthly Cattle Report, The Monthly Cattle On Feed Report and The Monthly Cold Storage Report. The important time period for these reports is winter through early spring.

LIVE CATTLE TRADE #1

Mega-Seasonals Live Cattle Trade #1 begins and ends with the Cattle On Feed Reports of December and March respectively. Demand for beef increases after the Thanksgiving holiday, as people get tired of turkey. This also is the time period that bad weather conditions limit cattle marketings. Thus we have an increased demand not met by an increased supply. The April Live Cattle Seasonal chart shows a very strong upward trend from November through March. This trade has produced profits of $31,330 in the last 20 years and been profitable in 82% of the years traded.

PERFORMANCE HISTORY (1978-1997)

Total Profit $31,330
Total Years Examined 20
Profit Years 14 (82%)
Loss Years 3 (18%)
Inactive Years 3
Average Profit $2,374
Average Loss $637
Profit-to-Loss Ratio 3.7
Total Profits/Total Losses 17.4

APRIL LIVE CATTLE
1978-1997

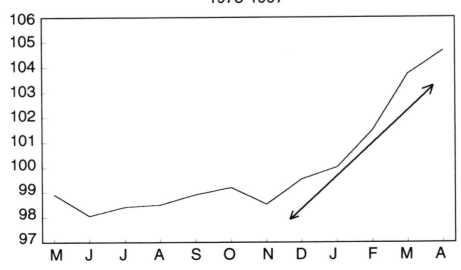

Rules for Live Cattle Trade #1

1. Enters long April Live Cattle from the second trading day of December through the last trading day of January.

2. Place a long entry stop 1 tick (2 1/2 points) above the high of the last 21 trading days. Move this stop as necessary.

3. When your order is filled, place a protective stop 1 tick (2 1/2 points) below the low of the last 2 trading days.

4. When the low of the last 21 trading days is equal to or greater than your long entry price, move your stop to 1 tick below the low of the last 21 trading days. Continue raising this stop as needed.

5. Exit this trade on the close of the first trading day after March 24th.

Historical Results for Live Cattle Trade #1
April Live Cattle

LCJ	ENTRY DATE	L/S	PRICE	EXIT DATE	EXIT METHOD	PRICE	TRADE P/L	YEARLY P/L
1978	12/05/77	L	40.025	03/27/78	DATEX	53.975	$ 5,580	$ 5,580
1979	12/04/78	L	61.000	03/26/79	DATEX	74.950	$ 5,580	$ 5,580
1980	N/T						$ N/T	$ N/T
1981	N/T						$ N/T	$ N/T
1982	01/11/82	L	59.275	03/25/82	DATEX	67.625	$ 3,340	$ 3,340
1983	12/21/82	L	59.125	03/25/83	DATEX	67.275	$ 4,060	$ 4,060
1984	12/07/83	L	65.875	01/25/84	PSTOP	66.625	$ 300	$ 300
1985	01/29/85	L	68.600	02/12/85	PROTS	67.125	$ (590)	$ (590)
1986	01/27/86	L	64.000	01/30/86	PROTS	61.950	$ (820)	$ (820)
1987	01/07/87	L	57.600	03/25/87	DATEX	67.950	$ 4,140	$ 4,140
1988	12/30/87	L	65.025	03/04/88	PSTOP	70.025	$ 2,000	$ 2,000
1989	12/21/88	L	75.325	01/18/89	PROTS	74.600	$ (290)	
	01/30/89	L	76.200	03/27/89	DATEX	78.150	$ 780	$ 490
1990	12/26/89	L	75.100	02/21/90	PSTOP	75.900	$ 320	$ 320
1991	12/10/90	L	76.775	01/09/91	PROTS	75.700	$ (430)	
	01/24/91	L	77.300	03/25/91	DATEX	80.650	$ 1,340	$ 910
1992	01/10/92	L	74.850	03/25/92	DATEX	77.725	$ 1,150	$ 1,150
1993	12/07/92	L	74.700	03/25/93	DATEX	82.775	$ 3,230	$ 3,230
1994	01/07/94	L	76.275	02/03/94	PROTS	75.025	$ (500)	$ (500)
1995	12/12/94	L	70.225	02/02/95	PSTOP	73.050	$ 1,130	$ 1,130
1996	N/T						$ N/T	$ N/T
1997	12/26/96	L	65.575	03/25/97	DATEX	68.100	$ 1,010	$ 1,010
1998	N/T						$ N/T	$ N/T

TOTAL $ 31,330

Exit Legend:

DATEX = Exit Date
PROTS = Protective Stop
PSTOP = Profit Stop
REV   = Reverse Entry

- Chapter 5 -

COCOA

Futures on the cocoa bean (10 metric tons) began trading on what is now the Coffee, Sugar and Cocoa Exchange back in 1925. In 1986, options on Cocoa futures began trading. The London International Financial Futures and Options Exchange (LIFFE) is the second largest Cocoa futures exchange.

Cocoa occasionally has long term trends, the cause of which is the long lag time it takes to adjust supply and demand. It takes four to five years from the planting of a cocoa tree until that tree enters into commercial production.

In the short run, both supply and demand are not very elastic. The supply of available cocoa beans is the October 1st carryover plus production. The Ivory Coast is the largest producer of cocoa. There are two harvests yearly. The "Main" crop year is October through March. The second crop, or "Mid-Crop" year is May through June. There are large Main crop shipments from November through the March/April time period. When trading cocoa, one should be aware of the weather on the Ivory Coast of Africa and also be alert to any potential dock strikes which can delay cocoa shipping.

Demand for cocoa is driven by price, which is quoted worldwide in British Pounds. A rapid or extreme change in the price of the British Pound can either increase or decrease some of the demand for cocoa. Candy manufacturers have a major influence on the demand side of the price equation.

Reports on Cocoa are issued by the International Cocoa Organization. The European Grindings Report is a surrogate for a cocoa demand report. By the way, "grindings" is the industry term for the process of turning cocoa beans into chocolate.

COCOA TRADE #1

Cocoa Trade #1 is a classic harvest time price decline. As the Main Cocoa Crop comes to market, prices are driven lower. The producers are hedging (selling) their crops and the users are lifting (selling) their long hedges. July Cocoa prices decline from a December/January rally to a bottoming out during June/July, as shown on the July Cocoa Seasonal Chart. This trade has produced profits of $21,580 since 1981.

PERFORMANCE HISTORY (1981-1997)

Total Profit..$21,580
Total Years Examined 17
Profit Years 11 (85%)
Loss Years 2 (15%)
Inactive Years 4
Average Profit...$2,113
Average Loss $830
Profit-to-Loss Ratio 2.5
Total Profits/Total Losses...........................14.0

JULY COCOA

1981-1997

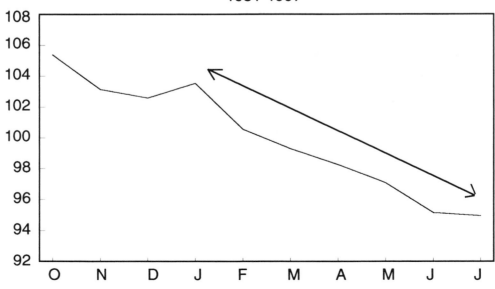

Rules for Cocoa Trade #1

1. Enters short July Cocoa from the second trading day of January through the last trading day of January.

2. Place a short entry stop 1 tick below the low of the last 15 trading days. Move this stop as needed.

3. When your order is filled, place a protective buy stop 1 tick above the high of the last 5 trading days.

4. When the high of the last 10 trading days is equal to or less than your entry price, lower your stop to 1 tick above the 10 day high. Lower this stop when necessary.

5. Exit trade on the close of the first trading day after June 21st.

Historical Results for Cocoa Trade #1
July Cocoa

CCN	ENTRY DATE	L/S	PRICE	EXIT DATE	EXIT METHOD	PRICE	TRADE P/L	YEARLY P/L
1981	01/13/81	S	2045	06/22/81	DATEX	1365	$ 6,800	$ 6,800
1982	01/25/82	S	2059	04/26/82	PSTOP	1720	$ 3,390	$ 3,390
1983	N/T						$ N/T	$ N/T
1984	01/10/84	S	2429	06/22/84	DATEX	2258	$ 1,710	$ 1,710
1985	N/T						$ N/T	$ N/T
1986	01/08/86	S	2259	03/13/86	PSTOP	2104	$ 1,550	$ 1,550
1987	01/23/87	S	1904	04/16/87	PROTS	2013	$ (1,090)	$ (1,090)
1988	01/27/88	S	1885	04/20/88	PSTOP	1594	$ 2,910	$ 2,910
1989	01/10/89	S	1389	05/19/89	PSTOP	1189	$ 2,000	$ 2,000
1990	N/T						$ N/T	$ N/T
1991	01/08/91	S	1219	01/10/91	PROTS	1241	$ (220)	
	01/30/91	S	1203	05/30/91	PSTOP	1008	$ 1,950	$ 1,730
1992	01/03/92	S	1302	03/19/92	PSTOP	1107	$ 1,950	$ 1,950
1993	01/26/93	S	980	02/22/93	PSTOP	968	$ 120	$ 120
1994	01/05/94	S	1197	02/18/94	PSTOP	1158	$ 390	$ 390
1995	N/T						$ N/T	$ N/T
1996	01/03/96	S	1299	01/15/96	PROTS	1322	$ (230)	
	01/31/96	S	1290	02/06/96	PROTS	1324	$ (340)	$ (570)
1997	01/09/97	S	1398	02/26/97	PSTOP	1329	$ 690	$ 690

TOTAL $ 21,580

Exit Legend:

DATEX = Exit Date
PROTS = Protective Stop
PSTOP = Profit Stop
REV   = Reverse Entry

- Chapter 6 -

COFFEE

Coffee futures are one of the oldies. Trading began in 1927 on the New York Coffee Exchange. Presently it trades on the New York Coffee, Sugar and Cocoa Exchange, Inc. Options on coffee futures are also traded and have good daily volume. Possibly the first people to use coffee were the ancient Ethiopians. Use of coffee spread through the various Arabian countries and by the 17th century Europeans were avid coffee drinkers.

Coffee is the most commercially valuable beverage grown in the world. Central and South America produce nearly 80% of the world's coffee, with Brazil producing the most. The weather in these areas has a considerable effect on the price of coffee. This is especially true of frosts. Frost is the mortal enemy of the coffee crop. One cold night can reverse the direction of the Coffee market, often with huge moves. Traders in the Coffee market must have both steady nerves and very well margined accounts.

The demand for coffee is stable, although extremely high prices have been known to create consumer resistance.

Reports that the Coffee trader should watch are the stockpile reports from the Green Coffee Association, the Coffee, Sugar and Cocoa Exchange warehouse stocks reports and Brazilian weather reports.

COFFEE TRADE #1

Mega-Seasonals Coffee Trade #1 is designed to enter the Coffee market during the time of the year that Brazil might experience freezes. Freezing temperatures do great damage to the coffee crop. Commercial users have already done their buying in the market to avoid possible steep price increases which a freeze could ignite. With commercials no longer buying coffee, prices fall. The September Coffee Seasonal Chart exhibits a downward trend from June through August that proves quite profitable. This trade has earned $97,975 since 1977. Be careful! This trade is potentially dangerous and should be traded by those with well margined accounts only! Normally Mega-Seasonal's unique entry method only allows entry when this danger is minimal.

PERFORMANCE HISTORY (1977-1997)

Total Profit $97,975
Total Years Examined 21
Profit Years 15 (85%)
Loss Years 3 (15%)
Inactive Years 3
Average Profit $6,991
Average Loss $2,296
Profit-to-Loss Ratio 3.0
Total Profits/Total Losses 15.2

SEPTEMBER COFFEE

1977-1997

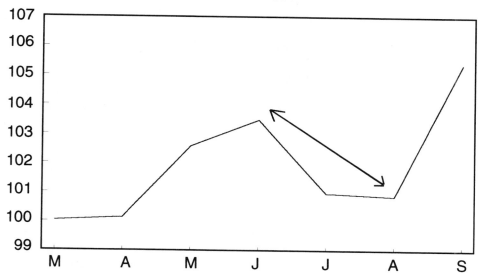

Rules for Coffee Trade #1

1. Enters short September Coffee from June 1st through August 1st.

2. Place a short entry stop 5 points below the low of the last 25 trading days. Raise this entry stop as necessary.

3. When filled, place a protective buy stop 5 points above the high of the last 2 trading days.

4. When the high of the last 9 trading days is equal to or less than the entry price, lower your stop to 5 points above the 9-day high. Lower this stop as the 9-day high declines.

5. Exit trade on the close of the first trading day after August 4th.

Historical Results for Coffee Trade #1
September Coffee

KCU	ENTRY DATE	L/S	PRICE	EXIT DATE	EXIT METHOD	PRICE	TRADE P/L	YEARLY P/L
1977	06/02/77	S	264.00	08/05/77	DATEX	188.50	$ 28,312	$ 28,312
1978	06/22/78	S	144.75	07/31/78	PSTOP	127.00	$ 6,656	$ 6,656
1979	07/27/79	S	200.39	08/06/79	DATEX	194.50	$ 2,209	$ 2,209
1980	06/10/80	S	196.50	08/05/80	DATEX	144.12	$ 19,643	$ 19,643
1981	06/01/81	S	111.00	07/06/81	PSTOP	96.07	$ 5,599	$ 5,599
1982	07/07/82	S	123.00	08/05/82	PROTS	130.55	$ (2,831)	$ (2,831)
1983	N/T							
1984	06/04/84	S	142.96	06/07/84	PROTS	145.95	$ (1,121)	
	06/19/84	S	141.20	06/27/84	PROTS	144.65	$ (1,294)	
	07/11/84	S	140.10	08/06/84	DATEX	139.78	$ 120	$ (2,295)
1985	06/21/85	S	143.45	08/05/85	DATEX	132.43	$ 4,133	$ 4,133
1986	06/01/86	S	189.00	07/11/86	PSTOP	173.85	$ 5,681	$ 5,681
1987	06/02/87	S	115.45	07/20/87	PSTOP	106.75	$ 3,263	$ 3,263
1988	06/29/88	S	132.10	07/07/88	PROTS	134.90	$ (1,050)	
	07/27/88	S	130.30	08/05/88	DATEX	115.79	$ 5,441	$ 4,391
1989	06/12/89	S	120.20	08/07/89	DATEX	82.50	$ 14,138	$ 14,138
1990	06/14/90	S	91.70	07/05/90	PSTOP	91.50	$ 75	
	07/13/90	S	84.75	07/26/90	PROTS	89.65	$ (1,838)	$ (1,763)
1991	06/07/91	S	88.15	06/25/91	PSTOP	87.45	$ 263	
	06/27/91	S	85.60	08/05/91	DATEX	82.90	$ 1,013	$ 1,276
1992	06/19/92	S	61.55	07/07/92	PSTOP	60.45	$ 413	
	07/27/92	S	56.75	08/05/92	DATEX	56.60	$ 56	$ 469
1993	N/T							
1994	N/T							
1995	06/07/95	S	151.95	07/14/95	PSTOP	141.80	$ 3,806	$ 3,806
1996	07/12/96	S	111.75	08/02/96	PSTOP	108.05	$ 1,388	$ 1,388
1997	06/11/97	S	188.45	07/23/97	PSTOP	178.05	$ 3,900	$ 3,900

TOTAL $ 97,975

Exit Legend:

DATEX = Date Exit
PROTS = Protective Stop
PSTOP = Profit Stop
REV   = Reverse Entry

COFFEE TRADE #2

Mega-Seasonals Coffee Trade #2 profits from the seasonal low in South American Coffee supplies. August is just prior to harvest and just before the increased seasonal demand. During this time the December Coffee market is usually spooked into a profitable rally. You can see this from the seasonal chart. Note the rally that begins in late July/early August and tops out in early September (harvest time in Brazil). Mega-Seasonals Coffee Trade #2 has earned excellent profits of $36,485 from this relatively short-term trade.

PERFORMANCE HISTORY (1977-1997)

Total Profit $36,485
Total Years Examined 21
Profit Years 15 (83%)
Loss Years 3 (17%)
Inactive Years 3
Average Profit $3,083
Average Loss $3,253
Profit-to-Loss Ratio 0.9
Total Profits/Total Losses 4.7

DECEMBER COFFEE
1977-1997

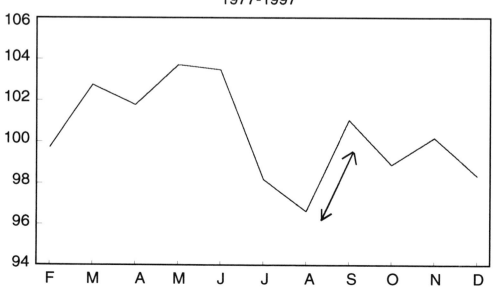

Rules for Coffee Trade #2

1. Enters long December Coffee from the first trading day of August to the first trading day of September.

2. Place a long entry stop 1 tick above the high of the last 13 trading days. As this high declines, lower this entry stop.

3. When filled, place a protective sell stop 1 tick below the low of the last 3 trading days.

4. When the low of the last 5 trading days is equal to or greater than the entry price, raise your stop to 1 tick below the 5-day low. As this 5-day low increases, raise your stop price.

5. Exit trade on the close of the first trading day after September 6th.

Historical Results for Coffee Trade #2
December Coffee

KCZ	ENTRY DATE	L/S	PRICE	EXIT DATE	EXIT METHOD	PRICE	TRADE P/L	YEARLY P/L
1977	08/25/77	L	196.61	08/26/77	PROTS	186.50	$ (3,791)	$ (3,791)
1978	08/09/78	L	121.31	09/07/78	DATEX	148.38	$ 10,151	$ 10,151
1979	08/15/79	L	194.01	09/07/79	DATEX	205.59	$ 4,343	$ 4,343
1980	N/T						$ N/T	$ N/T
1981	N/T						$ N/T	$ N/T
1982	08/04/82	L	119.30	08/25/82	PSTOP	123.60	$ 1,613	
	08/31/82	L	127.51	09/07/82	DATEX	130.95	$ 1,290	$ 2,903
1983	08/10/83	L	127.31	08/29/83	PSTOP	129.59	$ 855	$ 855
1984	08/09/84	L	139.96	09/04/84	PSTOP	144.10	$ 1,553	$ 1,553
1985	08/09/85	L	138.01	08/29/85	PSTOP	138.09	$ 30	$ 30
1986	08/19/86	L	183.91	09/08/86	DATEX	200.81	$ 6,338	$ 6,338
1987	08/07/87	L	110.96	09/08/87	DATEX	115.54	$ 1,718	$ 1,718
1988	08/19/88	L	124.16	09/07/88	DATEX	131.00	$ 2,565	$ 2,565
1989	08/29/89	L	84.86	09/07/89	DATEX	85.88	$ 383	$ 383
1990	08/13/90	L	98.36	09/05/90	PSTOP	100.24	$ 705	$ 705
1991	08/26/91	L	86.31	09/09/91	DATEX	93.55	$ 2,715	$ 2,715
1992	N/T						$ N/T	$ N/T
1993	08/02/93	L	80.60	08/11/93	PROTS	75.09	$ (2,066)	$ (2,066)
1994	08/26/94	L	199.51	09/07/94	DATEX	216.45	$ 6,353	$ 6,353
1995	08/16/95	L	147.00	08/30/95	PSTOP	150.79	$ 1,421	$ 1,421
1996	08/08/96	L	104.01	08/29/96	PSTOP	115.24	$ 4,211	$ 4,211
1997	08/06/97	L	176.31	08/15/97	PROTS	160.49	$ (6,033)	
	09/02/97	L	181.75	09/08/97	DATEX	187.70	$ 2,131	$ (3,902)

TOTAL $ 36,485

Exit Legend:

DATEX = Date Exit
PROTS = Protective Stop
PSTOP = Profit Stop
REV   = Reverse Entry

COFFEE TRADE #3

September is an interesting month for trading December Coffee. The "new crop" is harvested in South America and the producers are already looking ahead to next year's crop. During this time of the year producers are praying for rain. Their prayers are usually answered and the price of December Coffee drops. Although Mega-Seasonals Coffee Trade #3 does not enter the market every year, it has produced $57,430 in profits in the 16 years it has traded.

PERFORMANCE HISTORY (1977-1997)

Total Profit $57,430
Total Years Examined 21
Profit Years 12 (75%)
Loss Years 4 (25%)
Inactive Years 5
Average Profit $5,160
Average Loss $1,122
Profit-to-Loss Ratio 4.6
Total Profits/Total Losses 13.8

DECEMBER COFFEE

1977-1997

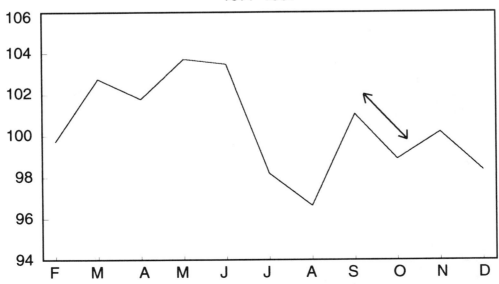

Rules for Coffee Trade #3

1. Enters short December Coffee from the 2nd trading day of September through the first trading day of October.

2. Place a short entry stop 1 tick below the low of the last 13 trading days. Move this stop as needed.

3. When filled, place a protective buy stop 1 tick above the high of the last 3 trading days.

4. When the high of the last 10 trading days is equal to or less than the entry price, lower your stop to 1 tick above the 10 day high. Lower this stop when necessary

5. Exit trade on the close of the first trading day after November 19th.

Historical Results for Coffee Trade #3
December Coffee

KCZ	ENTRY DATE	L/S	PRICE	EXIT DATE	EXIT METHOD	PRICE	TRADE P/L	YEARLY P/L
1977	09/07/77	S	178.00	09/19/77	PROTS	187.01	$ (3,379)	
	09/23/77	S	174.99	10/26/77	PSTOP	164.75	$ 3,840	$ 461
1978	N/T						$ N/T	$ N/T
1979	N/T						$ N/T	$ N/T
1980	09/03/80	S	130.91	09/08/80	PROTS	138.41	$ (2,813)	
	09/15/80	S	129.50	11/20/80	DATEX	114.25	$ 5,719	$ 2,906
1981	N/T						$ N/T	$ N/T
1982	N/T						$ N/T	$ N/T
1983	09/08/83	S	128.74	09/09/83	PROTS	130.41	$ (626)	$ (626)
1984	09/10/84	S	143.29	10/16/84	PSTOP	136.91	$ 2,393	$ 2,393
1985	09/04/85	S	137.04	10/10/85	PROTS	139.81	$ (1,039)	$ (1,039)
1986	10/01/86	S	196.50	11/20/86	DATEX	146.61	$ 18,709	$ 18,709
1987	09/22/87	S	113.00	10/01/87	PROTS	116.91	$ (1,466)	$ (1,466)
1988	N/T						$ N/T	$ N/T
1989	09/13/89	S	79.29	10/20/89	PSTOP	72.76	$ 2,449	$ 2,449
1990	09/12/90	S	96.64	11/20/90	DATEX	82.70	$ 5,228	$ 5,228
1991	09/27/91	S	87.09	10/16/91	PSTOP	82.01	$ 1,905	$ 1,905
1992	09/09/92	S	52.24	09/18/92	PROTS	55.86	$ (1,358)	$ (1,358)
1993	09/27/93	S	76.99	10/18/93	PSTOP	76.50	$ 184	$ 184
1994	09/30/94	S	207.99	11/21/94	DATEX	158.65	$ 18,503	$ 18,503
1995	09/07/95	S	143.30	10/16/95	PSTOP	124.76	$ 6,953	$ 6,953
1996	09/06/96	S	110.49	10/02/96	PSTOP	107.26	$ 1,211	$ 1,211
1997	09/18/97	S	167.49	09/19/97	PROTS	175.76	$ (3,101)	
	09/23/97	S	166.49	11/10/97	PSTOP	155.51	$ 4,118	$ 1,017

TOTAL $ 57,430

Exit Legend:

DATEX = Date Exit
PROTS = Protective Stop
PSTOP = Profit Stop
REV   = Reverse Entry

- Chapter 7 -

COPPER

The COMEX Division of the New York Mercantile Exchange has been trading futures on High Grade Copper since 1988. Before that a different specification of the Copper contract was traded. Options on High Grade Copper Futures began trading in 1988 and are at present quite active. Chile is the world's largest supplier of copper. This position was once held by the United States. Traders often call copper the "red metal."

The main factors affecting supply/production are regional labor problems, political problems and problems with governmental agencies and regulations.

Most copper is used in the manufacture of durable goods and in new home construction. The demand for both of these is a direct result of current economic trends and conditions. When the economy is doing well, new home starts are high and people are feeling confident; the demand for copper will be high. Should these factors reverse, the demand for copper will decrease.

The reports to watch when trading copper are the London Metal Exchange Copper Stocks Report, the New Housing Starts Report, Industrial Production, Gross Domestic Product Report, and Durable Goods Orders. Any surprises in the London Metal Exchange (LME) Stocks Report can easily reverse the direction of copper prices.

COPPER TRADE #1

The May/June time period is pivotal for September Copper. Will auto sales and housing starts improve, thereby increasing demand? If increased demand for the red metal does not materialize, copper prices will drop. This is why Mega-Seasonals Copper Trade #1 enters on either side of the market. The September Copper Seasonal Chart shows a very distinct downtrend from April through July. This is somewhat misleading as there is occasionally a strong counter-seasonal trend. Copper Trade #1 has traded all 21 of the last 21 years for a profit of $26,000.

PERFORMANCE HISTORY (1977-1997)

Total Profit...$26,000
Total Years Examined 21
Profit Years 15 (71%)
Loss Years 6 (29%)
Inactive Years 0
Average Profit...$1,956
Average Loss $557
Profit-to-Loss Ratio 3.5
Total Profits/Total Losses............................. 8.8

SEPTEMBER COPPER
1977-1997

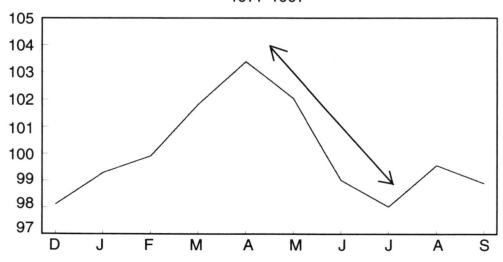

Rules for Copper Trade #1:

1. Enters long and short September Copper from the second trading day of May through the first trading day of July.

2. Place a long entry stop 5 points (1 tick) above the high of the last 40 trading days. Place a short entry stop 5 points (1 tick) under the low of the last 40 trading days. Move these entry stops as the 40 day high and low change.

3. When filled:
   On long: Place a protective sell stop 20 points under the low of the last two trading days.
   On short: Place a protective buy stop 20 points above the high of the last two trading days.

   Remember to continue entering the opposite entry described in #2 above, until you are no longer in the trade entry time period. Should you already have entered a trade via #2 and the reverse entry price is greater than either your protective sell stop or profit stop (for longs), use the entry price to exit the current trade so that your new position is short. Of course, should you presently be short, adjust the protective buy stop or profit stop.

4. If long: When the low of the last 19 trading days is equal to or greater than the long entry price, raise your stop to 5 points under the 19 day low.
   If short: When the high of the last 19 trading days is equal to or less than the short entry price, lower your stop to 5 points above the 19 day high.
   Remember to change the stop as necessary.

5. Exit this trade on the close of the first trading day after July 5th.

Historical Results for Copper Trade #1
September Hi-Grade (COMEX) Copper

HGU	ENTRY DATE	L/S	PRICE	EXIT DATE	EXIT METHOD	PRICE	TRADE P/L		YEARLY P/L	
1977	05/19/77	S	64.05	07/06/77	DATEX	58.20	$	1,463	$	1,463
1978	05/25/78	L	64.55	06/13/78	PROTS	63.00	$	(388)		
	06/28/78	S	59.75	07/06/78	DATEX	60.20	$	(113)	$	(501)
1979	05/11/79	S	84.90	07/06/79	DATEX	80.75	$	1,038	$	1,038
1980	06/10/80	S	88.00	06/27/80	PROTS	92.00	$	(1,000)	$	(1,000)
1981	05/04/81	S	84.95	07/06/81	DATEX	76.50	$	2,113	$	2,113
1982	05/04/82	L	75.30	05/18/82	PROTS	72.90	$	(600)		
	05/19/82	S	70.00	07/06/82	DATEX	60.10	$	2,475	$	1,875
1983	05/03/83	L	81.65	05/20/83	PROTS	79.05	$	(650)		
	06/01/83	S	76.80	07/06/83	DATEX	76.30	$	125	$	(525)
1984	05/07/84	S	66.15	07/06/84	DATEX	58.70	$	1,863	$	1,863
1985	05/30/85	S	61.80	07/09/85	DATEX	60.10	$	425	$	425
1986	05/20/86	S	62.65	06/06/86	PROTS	64.30	$	(413)		
	06/24/86	S	62.00	07/07/86	DATEX	59.70	$	575	$	162
1987	05/06/87	L	64.35	07/06/87	DATEX	74.85	$	2,625	$	2,625
1988	06/03/88	L	96.55	07/06/88	DATEX	95.50	$	(263)	$	(263)
1989	05/15/89	S	115.00	07/06/89	DATEX	98.80	$	4,050	$	4,050
1990	05/09/90	L	111.55	06/26/90	PROTS	105.25	$	(1,575)	$	
	06/28/90	L	112.55	07/06/90	DATEX	118.20	$	1,413	$	(162)
1991	05/03/91	S	103.40	06/11/91	PSTOP	99.75	$	913	$	913
1992	06/02/92	L	102.65	07/06/92	DATEX	111.65	$	2,250	$	2,250
1993	05/04/93	S	83.05	06/04/93	PROTS	86.80	$	(938)		
	07/01/93	L	87.15	07/06/93	DATEX	87.35	$	50	$	(888)
1994	05/06/94	L	93.35	07/06/94	DATEX	111.35	$	4,500	$	4,500
1995	05/02/95	S	122.40	05/23/95	PROTS	125.70	$	(825)		
	06/01/95	L	130.05	07/06/95	DATEX	135.85	$	1,450	$	625
1996	05/03/96	L	119.05	05/17/96	PROTS	117.00	$	(513)		
	05/20/96	S	110.55	07/08/96	DATEX	90.55	$	5,000	$	4,487
1997	05/08/97	L	108.35	06/24/97	PSTOP	112.15	$	950	$	950

TOTAL $ 26,000

Exit Legend:

DATEX = Exit Date
PROTS = Protective Stop
PSTOP = Profit Stop
REV   = Reverse Entry

COPPER TRADE #2

Declining world warehouse stocks is often the catalyst to a seasonal price rise in March Copper from the October/November time frame to January/February. The March Copper Seasonal Chart exhibits this uptrend. This Mega-Seasonals trade has generated $23,940 in profits since 1977.

PERFORMANCE HISTORY (1977-1998)

Total Profit...$23,940
Total Years Examined 22
Profit Years 12 (67%)
Loss Years 6 (33%)
Inactive Years 4
Average Profit...$2,341
Average Loss $692
Profit-to-Loss Ratio 3.4
Total Profits/Total Losses 6.8

MARCH COPPER
1977-1997

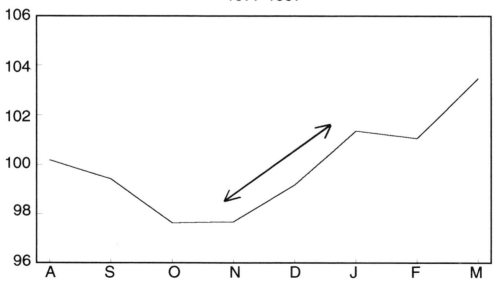

Rules for Copper Trade #2:

1. Enters long March Copper from the first trading day after November 10th through the first trading day of January.

2. Place a long entry stop 50 points above the high of the last 12 trading days. Move this stop as necessary.

3. When filled, place a protective sell stop 10 points below the low of the last 2 trading days.

4. When the low of the last 16 trading days is equal to or greater than the entry price, raise your stop to 5 points (1 tick) under the 16 day low. Raise this stop as the 16 day low increases.

5. Exit this trade on the close of the first trading day after February 24th.

Historical Results for Copper Trade #2
March Hi-Grade (COMEX) Copper

HGH	ENTRY DATE	L/S	PRICE	EXIT DATE	EXIT METHOD	PRICE	TRADE P/L	YEARLY P/L
1977	12/15/76	L	60.30	02/10/77	PSTOP	64.55	$ 1,063	$ 1,063
1978	11/17/77	L	57.30	01/17/78	PSTOP	58.60	$ 325	$ 325
1979	12/04/78	L	69.70	02/26/79	DATEX	88.10	$ 4,600	$ 4,600
1980	11/16/79	L	99.50	11/27/79	PROTS	95.10	$ (1,100)	
	11/30/79	L	102.30	02/20/80	PSTOP	123.70	$ 5,350	$ 4,250
1981	N/T						$ N/T	$ N/T
1982	12/02/81	L	78.35	12/09/81	PROTS	74.90	$ (863)	$ (863)
1983	11/30/82	L	67.30	02/25/83	DATEX	78.65	$ 2,838	$ 2,838
1984	11/22/83	L	65.95	12/15/83	PROTS	63.70	$ (563)	$ (563)
1985	N/T						$ N/T	$ N/T
1986	12/05/85	L	63.30	02/03/86	PSTOP	64.40	$ 275	$ 275
1987	11/28/86	L	61.15	02/25/87	DATEX	63.35	$ 550	$ 550
1988	11/18/87	L	95.50	01/13/88	PSTOP	110.85	$ 3,838	$ 3,838
1989	11/22/88	L	123.30	02/03/89	PSTOP	134.45	$ 2,788	$ 2,788
1990	12/22/89	L	106.50	01/15/90	PROTS	104.10	$ (600)	$ (600)
1991	12/20/90	L	110.70	01/15/91	PROTS	107.50	$ (800)	$ (800)
1992	N/T						$ N/T	$ N/T
1993	11/27/92	L	98.60	01/12/93	PSTOP	98.50	$ (25)	$ (25)
1994	12/01/93	L	76.40	02/11/94	PSTOP	84.40	$ 2,000	$ 2,000
1995	11/14/94	L	124.75	02/01/95	PSTOP	135.00	$ 2,563	$ 2,563
1996	12/14/95	L	126.50	12/26/95	PROTS	121.30	$ (1,300)	$ (1,300)
1997	11/12/96	L	94.70	12/16/96	PSTOP	96.95	$ 563	
	01/02/97	L	101.70	02/25/97	DATEX	111.45	$ 2,438	$ 3,001
1998	N/T						$ N/T	$ N/T

TOTAL $ 23,940

Exit Legend:

DATEX = Exit Date
PROTS = Protective Stop
PSTOP = Profit Stop
REV   = Reverse Entry

- Chapter 8 -

CORN

It seems that Corn futures have been trading on the Chicago Board of Trade since time began, but actually trading began in 1877. The size of the Board of Trade Corn Futures contract is 5000 bu. The MidAmerica Commodity Exchange trades a smaller sized contract of 1000 bu. Options on corn futures are also traded. Corn is the most valuable single crop grown in the United States. It was the first crop to be planted as farmers moved westward into what is now the Midwest and West.

On the supply side of the supply/demand equation are the yearly carryover and spring planting intentions. Three quarters of all corn production is in the Corn Belt States of Iowa, Illinois, Minnesota, Indiana, Ohio, Missouri and South Dakota. Normally, the majority of the corn carryover is held in the hands or silos of farmers in these states. The weather conditions in these states during planting, growing and harvesting are of extreme importance. Drought during the growing season is the greatest threat to the corn crop. Too little rain during the growing and silking period can prompt a "Weather Market Rally." When this happens it is not unusual for new crop December corn to easily add 40% to 50% to its price in a relatively short period of time.

The demand for corn comes from various types of livestock feeding operations. The number of hogs and pigs, cattle and calves and poultry have a great bearing on the price of corn.

The major reports for the corn trader to watch are the Planting Intentions Report in the spring and the Crop Production Reports issued during the growing and harvesting time periods.

CORN TRADE #1

Corn Trade #1 has possibly the best fundamental supply/demand logic of all the trades. In the time period up to harvest, prices increase due to the drawdown of available carryover and fears about the condition and size of the "new" crop. The closer to harvest time, the more that is known about the crop. Farmers start their hedging operations (selling corn) and users begin lifting their long hedges (selling corn). As the December Corn Seasonal Chart shows, the selling has a great effect on the price of the December "new" corn. Mega-Seasonals Corn Trade #1 takes full advantage of this trend. Profits for this trade over the last 21 years have been $16,653.

PERFORMANCE HISTORY (1977-1997)

Total Profit...$16,653
Total Years Examined 21
Profit Years 16 (76%)
Loss Years 5 (24%)
Inactive Years 0
Average Profit...$1,213
Average Loss $550
Profit-to-Loss Ratio 2.2
Total Profits/Total Losses........................... 7.1

DECEMBER CORN
1977-1997

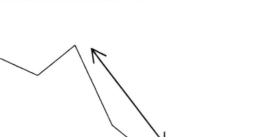

Rules for Corn Trade #1:

1. Enters short December Corn from May 16th through July 31st.

2. Place a short entry stop 2 cents below the low of the last 21 trading days.

3. When filled place a protective buy stop 1 tick (1/4 cent) above the high of the last 8 trading days.

4. When the high of the last 12 trading days is equal to or less than the entry price, lower your stop to 1 tick above the 12 day high. Moving this as necessary.

5. Exit this trade on the close of the first trading day after August 19th.

Historical Results for Corn Trade #1
December Corn

CZ	ENTRY DATE	L/S	PRICE	EXIT DATE	EXIT METHOD	PRICE		TRADE P/L		YEARLY P/L
1977	06/10/77	S	241.50	08/22/77	DATEX	191.00	$	2,525	$	2,525
1978	07/03/78	S	251.00	08/21/78	DATEX	228.25	$	1,138	$	1,138
1979	07/27/79	S	293.00	08/20/79	DATEX	281.75	$	563	$	563
1980	06/02/80	S	290.25	07/01/80	PROTS	300.75	$	(525)	$	(525)
1981	05/21/81	S	361.25	08/20/81	DATEX	314.75	$	2,325	$	2,325
1982	05/25/82	S	280.25	08/20/82	DATEX	228.00	$	2,613	$	2,613
1983	05/20/83	S	283.75	06/23/83	PSTOP	283.75	$	0	$	0
1984	07/11/84	S	291.75	08/20/84	DATEX	276.25	$	775	$	775
1985	05/20/85	S	256.75	08/20/85	DATEX	222.00	$	1,738	$	1,738
1986	06/12/86	S	190.50	08/20/86	DATEX	168.75	$	1,088	$	1,088
1987	07/01/87	S	187.00	08/20/87	DATEX	168.50	$	925	$	925
1988	07/20/88	S	307.00	08/22/88	DATEX	286.00	$	1,050	$	1,050
1989	05/17/89	S	252.25	06/14/89	PSTOP	244.50	$	388		
	07/18/89	S	237.00	08/11/89	PSTOP	235.75	$	63	$	451
1990	06/04/90	S	263.00	06/08/90	PROTS	282.00	$	(950)		
	07/09/90	S	269.75	08/20/90	DATEX	245.25	$	1,225	$	275
1991	06/17/91	S	238.00	07/24/91	PROTS	250.75	$	(638)	$	(638)
1992	07/06/92	S	249.00	08/20/92	DATEX	221.00	$	1,400	$	1,400
1993	06/01/93	S	232.75	07/01/93	PROTS	241.00	$	(413)	$	(413)
1994	06/22/94	S	247.25	08/08/94	PSTOP	223.25	$	1,200	$	1,200
1995	06/27/95	S	271.50	07/17/95	PROTS	295.00	$	(1,175)	$	(1,175)
1996	07/19/96	S	343.00	08/12/96	PSTOP	331.25	$	588	$	588
1997	05/20/97	S	261.00	07/14/97	PSTOP	246.00	$	750	$	750

TOTAL $ 16,653

Exit Legend:

DATEX = Exit Date
PROTS = Protective Stop
PSTOP = Profit Stop
REV   = Reverse Entry

- Chapter 9 -

COTTON

In the late 1940's the total value of Cotton futures traded was greater than the total value of equities traded on the New York Stock Exchange. Cotton futures began trading on the New York Cotton Exchange back in 1870. Options on Cotton futures have traded since 1984. Cotton is no longer as heavily traded as in the 1940's, but it still has tradeable volume. Over the years the U. S. has been losing its dominant position in the World Cotton Market.

The supply side of the cotton market is determined by world carryover, planting intentions and weather conditions in the various cotton producing areas. The South Central, the Southwest and the Western areas of the United States are the main cotton producing areas.

Cotton planting is usually completed by the end of May. From then until October, when the harvest begins, weather can be of utmost importance. Too much or too little rain can drive violent price action in the Cotton markets. That is why many traders have said that the Cotton market is one of the hardest from which to profit. Yet, Mega-Seasonals profits!

On the demand side of this equation is world consumption, substitute fabrics and exports. Often demand factors are of greater and longer term importance than supply factors.

The price of cotton responds to the Crop Production Report and the Cotton Consumption And Stock Report. These reports often cause limit moves. This characteristic of the Cotton market should restrict trading to only traders with well margined accounts.

COTTON TRADE #1

Cotton Trade #1 is based on pre-harvest price pressures. The further into the growing season you get, the greater the knowledge about the size and condition of the "new" cotton crop. This knowledge takes much of the doubt out of the market and planters start their hedging activities. Cotton users also know more about the crop and lift any long hedges they may have in place. The October Cotton Seasonal Chart demonstrates this decline from May to September. Mega-Seasonals Cotton Trade #1 profits from this seasonal down move to the tune of $32,745 in the last 21 years.

PERFORMANCE HISTORY (1977-1997)

Total Profit	$32,745
Total Years Examined	21
Profit Years	15 (83%)
Loss Years	3 (18%)
Inactive Years	3
Average Profit	$2,317
Average Loss	$672
Profit-to-Loss Ratio	3.4
Total Profits/Total Losses	17.3

OCTOBER COTTON
1977-1997

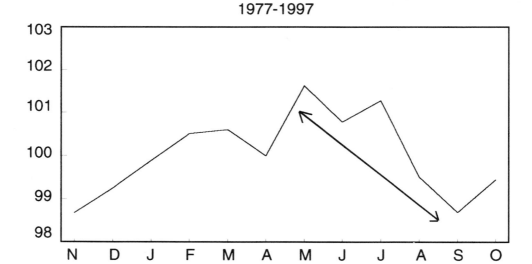

Rules for Cotton Trade #1:

1. Enters short October Cotton from June 15th through the last trading day of July.

2. Place a short entry stop 5 points (1 tick) below the low of the last 16 trading days. Raising this as needed.

3. When your order is filled, place a protective buy stop 5 points above the 5-day high.

4. When the high of the last 8 trading days is equal to or less than your short entry price, lower your stop to 5 points above the 8-day high. Keep lowering this stop as necessary.

5. Exit trade on the close of the first trading day after August 22nd.

Historical Results for Cotton Trade #1
October Cotton

CTV	ENTRY DATE	L/S	PRICE	EXIT DATE	EXIT METHOD	PRICE	TRADE P/L	YEARLY P/L
1977	07/08/77	S	59.80	08/23/77	DATEX	54.62	$ 2,590	$ 2,590
1978	06/27/78	S	60.75	07/14/78	PSTOP	60.45	$ 150	$ 150
1979	06/28/79	S	64.00	08/23/79	DATEX	63.65	$ 175	$ 175
1980	N/T						$ N/T	$ N/T
1981	06/29/81	S	78.05	07/06/81	PROTS	80.00	$ (975)	
	07/13/81	S	77.35	08/24/81	DATEX	66.00	$ 5,675	$ 4,700
1982	06/16/82	S	66.05	06/21/82	PROTS	67.90	$ (925)	
	07/26/82	S	70.10	08/23/82	DATEX	65.13	$ 2,485	$ 1,560
1983	07/01/83	S	76.50	08/23/83	DATEX	79.05	$ (1,275)	$ (1,275)
1984	06/18/84	S	74.45	08/03/84	PSTOP	67.50	$ 3,475	$ 3,475
1985	07/19/85	S	60.35	08/23/85	DATEX	57.73	$ 1,310	$ 1,310
1986	06/25/86	S	32.75	07/23/86	PSTOP	31.25	$ 750	$ 750
1987	N/T						$ N/T	$ N/T
1988	06/30/88	S	62.65	08/23/88	DATEX	50.40	$ 6,125	$ 6,125
1989	N/T						$ N/T	$ N/T
1990	07/10/90	S	75.05	08/23/90	DATEX	73.42	$ 815	$ 815
1991	06/25/91	S	76.62	07/23/91	PSTOP	71.45	$ 2,585	
	07/29/91	S	68.51	08/23/91	DATEX	64.20	$ 2,155	$ 4,740
1992	07/07/92	S	62.40	07/10/92	PROTS	64.60	$ (1,100)	
	07/27/92	S	62.25	08/24/92	DATEX	60.18	$ 1,035	$ (65)
1993	06/17/93	S	57.60	07/09/93	PROTS	58.95	$ (675)	$ (675)
1994	06/20/94	S	76.36	07/22/94	PSTOP	72.05	$ 2,155	$ 2,155
1995	07/05/95	S	84.65	08/14/95	PSTOP	75.12	$ 4,765	$ 4,765
1996	06/19/96	S	75.80	07/19/96	PSTOP	73.95	$ 925	$ 925
1997	07/07/97	S	74.15	08/25/97	DATEX	73.10	$ 525	$ 525

TOTAL $ 32,745

Exit Legend:

DATEX = Exit Date
PROTS = Protective Stop
PSTOP = Profit Stop
REV   = Reverse Entry

COTTON TRADE #2

Mega-Seasonals Cotton Trade #2 is based on demand. Once the cotton harvest is in, will the demand be strong enough to utilize the carryover plus the "new" crop, or not? Since the March Cotton Seasonal Chart shows a rally from December to March it would seem that the answer to this question is "yes." On further inspection, December is a pivotal month. Demand does not always meet the supply. That is why Cotton Trade #2 enters on both sides of the market. This trade has proven quite profitable. Over the last 22 years it has earned $43,640.

PERFORMANCE HISTORY (1977-1998)

Total Profit $43,640
Total Years Examined 22
Profit Years 15 (75%)
Loss Years 5 (25%)
Inactive Years 2
Average Profit $3,490
Average Loss $1,742
Profit-to-Loss Ratio 2.0
Total Profits/Total Losses 6.0

MARCH COTTON
1977 - 1998

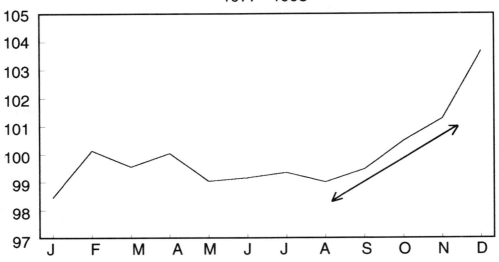

Rules for Cotton Trade #2:

1. Enters long and short March Cotton from December 1st through December 31st.

2. Place a long entry stop 25 points above the high of the last 24 trading days. Place a short entry stop 25 points below the low of the last 24 trading days. Change these entry stops as needed.

3. When filled:
   On long: Place a protective sell stop 5 points below the 4-day low.
   On short: Place a protective buy stop 5 points above the 4-day high.

   Remember to continue entering the opposite entry order, as described in #2 above, until you are no longer in the trade entry window. Should you already have entered a trade via #2, and the reverse entry price is greater than either your protective sell stop or profit stop (for longs), use the entry price to exit the current trade so that your new position is short. Of course, should you presently be short, adjust the protective buy stop or profit stop.

4. If long: When the low of the last 18 trade days is equal to or greater than your long entry price, raise your stop to 5 points below the 18 day low.
   If short: When the high of the last 18 trading days is equal to or less than the short entry price, lower your stop to 5 points above the 18 day high.
   Move as necessary.

5. Exit long position on the close of the first trading day of March.

   Exit short position on the close of the first trading day after January 11th.

Historical Results for Cotton Trade #2
March Cotton

CTH	ENTRY DATE	L/S	PRICE	EXIT DATE	EXIT METHOD	PRICE	TRADE P/L	YEARLY P/L
1977	12/13/76	S	77.69	01/12/77	DATEX	67.32	$ 5,185	$ 5,185
1978	12/19/77	L	53.10	02/13/78	PSTOP	53.95	$ 425	$ 425
1979	12/11/78	S	68.85	01/12/79	DATEX	65.25	$ 1,800	$ 1,800
1980	12/04/79	L	72.10	02/22/80	PSTOP	79.65	$ 3,775	$ 3,775
1981	12/05/80	L	93.00	12/12/80	PROTS	88.00	$ (2,500)	
	12/22/80	L	94.45	01/21/81	PROTS	90.46	$ (1,995)	$ (4,495)
1982	12/07/81	S	62.45	12/23/81	PROTS	64.50	$ (1,025)	
	12/28/81	L	65.75	02/12/82	PROTS	62.56	$ (1,595)	$ (2,620)
1983	12/09/82	L	66.65	03/01/83	DATEX	71.30	$ 2,325	$ 2,325
1984	12/15/83	S	78.80	01/12/84	DATEX	75.15	$ 1,825	$ 1,825
1985	N/T						$ N/T	$ N/T
1986	12/10/85	S	59.85	12/12/85	PROTS	60.98	$ (565)	$ (565)
1987	12/01/86	L	53.10	01/28/87	PSTOP	56.77	$ 1,835	$ 1,835
1988	12/04/87	S	65.60	01/12/88	DATEX	64.13	$ 735	$ 735
1989	12/02/88	L	57.35	02/09/89	PSTOP	58.04	$ 345	$ 345
1990	12/04/89	S	69.45	01/12/90	DATEX	66.15	$ 1,650	$ 1,650
1991	12/10/90	L	75.20	03/01/91	DATEX	88.10	$ 6,450	$ 6,450
1992	N/T						$ N/T	$ N/T
1993	12/04/92	L	59.15	03/01/93	DATEX	63.00	$ 1,925	$ 1,925
1994	12/03/93	L	63.70	03/01/94	DATEX	78.90	$ 7,600	$ 7,600
1995	12/01/94	L	80.70	03/01/95	DATEX	110.92	$ 15,110	$ 15,110
1996	12/19/95	S	82.27	01/12/96	DATEX	82.65	$ (190)	$ (190)
1997	12/02/96	L	76.38	12/04/96	PROTS	74.70	$ (840)	$ (840)
1998	12/02/97	S	69.80	12/31/97	OPEN	67.07	$ 1,365	$ 1,365

TOTAL $ 43,640

Exit Legend:

DATEX = Exit Date
PROTS = Protective Stop
PSTOP = Profit Stop
REV   = Reverse Entry

- Chapter 10 -

CRUDE OIL

Futures on Crude Oil (1000 barrels) began trading on the New York Mercantile Exchange in 1983. Options on these futures began trading in 1986. Both have outstanding liquidity. Crude Oil is the largest cash commodity in the world. Crude Oil's price and that of its two main products (gasoline and heating oil) can be exceedingly volatile.

Crude Oil is normally a demand driven market with one major exception, that of political upheaval. Government policies, regulations and disagreements can cause shortages that can in some cases make an already volatile market violent.

The demand for Crude Oil is primarily influenced by the demand for its major products, heating oil and gasoline. A shortage in the supply of either of these products at an inappropriate time of the year can have a dramatic effect on the price of crude oil.

The weekly American Petroleum Institutes (API) Report on inventories of crude oil, heating oil and gasoline is the petroleum futures trader's best friend. Should surprises happen, watch for rapid price changes.

CRUDE OIL TRADE #1

March is the time that many refineries switch their production emphasis from heating oil to gasoline. This frequently causes a shortage of heating oil inventories. Should there be a cold snap, heating oil prices will shoot up, pulling crude oil up with it. The June Crude Oil Seasonal Chart shows the result. Mega-Seasonals Crude Oil Trade #1 has pumped $14,690 in profits since 1984.

PERFORMANCE HISTORY (1984-1997)

Total Profit $14,690
Total Years Examined 14
Profit Years 9 (75%)
Loss Years 3 (25%)
Inactive Years 2
Average Profit $1,827
Average Loss $583
Profit-to-Loss Ratio 3.1
Total Profits/Total Losses 9.4

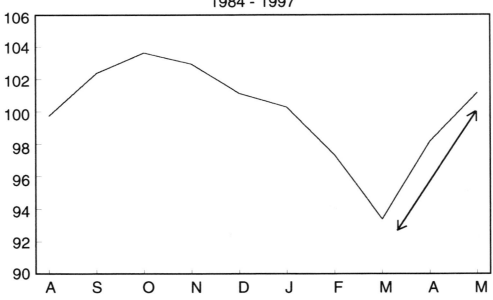

JUNE CRUDE OIL

1984 - 1997

Rules for Crude Oil Trade #1:

1. Enters long June Crude Oil from the first trading day of March through the second trading day of April.

2. Place a long entry stop 1 tick above the high of the last 16 trading days. As the 16 day high drops, lower your entry stop to 1 tick above the new 16 day high.

3. When filled, place a protective sell stop 1 tick below the low of the last 3 trading days.

4. When the low of the last 14 trading days is equal to or greater than the entry price, raise your sell stop to 1 tick below the 14 day low. Raise this stop as needed.

5. Exit this trade on the close of the first trading day after April 20th.

Historical Results for Crude Oil Trade #1
June Crude Oil

CLM	ENTRY DATE	L/S	PRICE	EXIT DATE	EXIT METHOD	PRICE	TRADE P/L	YEARLY P/L
1984	03/28/84	L	30.90	04/23/84	DATEX	30.57	$ (330)	$ (330)
1985	03/04/85	L	26.61	04/22/85	DATEX	28.49	$ 1,880	$ 1,880
1986	N/T						$ N/T	$ N/T
1987	03/09/87	L	18.01	04/21/87	DATEX	18.40	$ 390	$ 390
1988	03/21/88	L	16.40	04/21/88	DATEX	18.36	$ 1,960	$ 1,960
1989	03/01/89	L	17.51	04/21/89	DATEX	21.32	$ 3,770	$ 3,770
1990	N/T						$ N/T	$ N/T
1991	03/04/91	L	19.52	04/22/91	DATEX	21.32	$ 1,800	$ 1,800
1992	03/12/92	L	19.13	04/21/92	DATEX	20.44	$ 1,310	$ 1,310
1993	03/04/93	L	20.79	03/10/93	PROTS	20.47	$ (320)	$ (320)
1994	03/21/94	L	15.20	03/28/94	PROTS	14.54	$ (660)	
	04/04/94	L	15.39	04/21/94	DATEX	16.63	$ 1,240	$ 580
1995	03/20/95	L	18.40	04/21/95	DATEX	20.41	$ 2,010	$ 2,010
1996	03/12/96	L	18.79	04/21/96	DATEX	21.53	$ 2,740	$ 2,740
1997	03/17/97	L	21.16	04/02/97	PROTS	20.06	$ (1,100)	$ (1,100)

TOTAL $ 14,690

Exit Legend:

DATEX = Exit Date
PROTS = Protective Stop
PSTOP = Profit Stop
REV   = Reverse Entry

CRUDE OIL TRADE #2

The fundamentals behind Mega-Seasonals Crude Oil Trade #2 are the reverse of those for Crude Oil Trade #1. This is the time of the year when refineries are switching production emphasis from gasoline to heating oil. Supplies of heating oil are low at this time of the year. Orders from heating oil suppliers are coming in, and Labor Day driving is depleting gasoline supplies. With both of the major products of crude oil in demand, the price has nowhere to go but up (as the November Crude Oil Seasonal Chart shows). Mega-Seasonals Crude Oil Trade #2 has earned profits of $25,350 from this trade over the last 15 years.

PERFORMANCE HISTORY (1983-1997)

Total Profit $25,350
Total Years Examined 15
Profit Years 11 (73%)
Loss Years 4 (27%)
Inactive Years 0
Average Profit $2,429
Average Loss $343
Profit-to-Loss Ratio 7.1
Total Profits/Total Losses 19.5

NOVEMBER CRUDE OIL
1983 - 1997

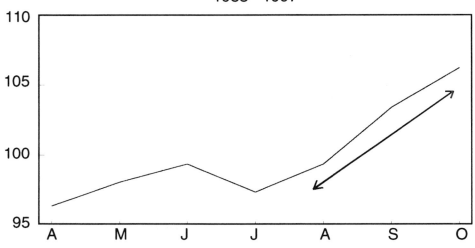

Rules for Crude Oil Trade #2:

1. Enters long November Crude Oil from the second trading day of August through the first trading day of September.

2. Place a long entry stop 1 tick above the high of the last 5 trading days. Move this entry stop when necessary.

3. When filled, place a protective sell stop 1 tick under the low of the last 3 trading days.

4. When the low of the last eight trading days is equal to or greater than the entry price, raise your sell stop to 1 tick below the 8-day low. Raise this stop as needed.

5. Exit this trade on the close of the first trading day after September 26th.

Historical Results for Crude Oil Trade #2
November Crude Oil

CLX	ENTRY DATE	L/S	PRICE	EXIT DATE	EXIT METHOD	PRICE	TRADE P/L	YEARLY P/L
1983	08/02/83	L	32.16	08/19/83	PROTS	31.64	$ (520)	$ (520)
1984	08/02/84	L	28.64	08/30/84	PSTOP	29.52	$ 880	$ 880
1985	08/07/85	L	26.52	09/05/85	PSTOP	27.42	$ 900	$ 900
1986	08/04/86	L	11.91	09/08/86	PSTOP	15.52	$ 3,610	$ 3,610
1987	08/27/87	L	19.40	09/28/87	DATEX	19.45	$ 50	$ 50
1988	08/22/88	L	16.03	08/23/88	PROTS	15.69	$ (340)	$ (340)
1989	08/10/89	L	18.10	09/22/89	PSTOP	19.23	$ 1,130	$ 1,130
1990	08/02/90	L	23.42	08/29/90	PSTOP	26.09	$ 2,670	
	09/04/90	L	28.07	09/27/90	DATEX	39.54	$ 11,470	$ 14,140
1991	08/09/91	L	21.48	09/06/91	PSTOP	21.59	$ 110	$ 110
1992	08/17/92	L	21.24	09/25/92	PSTOP	21.66	$ 420	$ 420
1993	08/11/93	L	18.39	09/01/93	PSTOP	18.39	$ 0	$ 0
1994	08/29/94	L	17.70	09/13/94	PROTS	17.19	$ (510)	$ (510)
1995	08/02/95	L	17.45	08/15/95	PROTS	17.08	$ (370)	
	08/21/95	L	17.42	09/21/95	PSTOP	17.97	$ 550	$ 180
1996	08/02/96	L	20.00	09/27/96	DATEX	24.60	$ 4,600	$ 4,600
1997	08/04/97	L	20.46	08/08/97	PROTS	19.84	$ (620)	
	09/02/97	L	19.94	09/29/97	DATEX	21.26	$ 1,320	$ 700

TOTAL $ 25,350

Exit Legend:

DATEX = Exit Date
PROTS = Protective Stop
PSTOP = Profit Stop

- Chapter 11 -

D-MARK

Futures on the German Currency, the Deutsche Mark, began trading on the International Monetary Market Division of the Chicago Mercantile Exchange in 1972. In 1984 options on D-Mark futures began trading. The IMM contract size is 125,000 D-Marks. A half-sized contract of 62,500 D-Marks trades on the MidAmerica Commodity Exchange.

The Mark is driven mostly by demand. The US/German Balance of Payments is of great importance when judging the value of the D-Mark versus that of the U. S. Dollar. The Balance of Payments has two components. The first, The Balance Of Trade, represents the difference between U. S. Exports to and from Germany. The second component is the Flow of Capital. The Flow of Capital represents the movement of investment funds. Investment opportunities, including interest rate differentials and financial market attractiveness, causes capital to flow between the two countries. Interest rates are the major controlling force used by the German Central Bank, the Bundesbank, to control inflation.

The German economic climate has a direct effect on the price of the D-Mark. The Bundsesbank has, on occasion, bought or sold D-Marks on the open market to influence the Mark's price. It is rare that a single government intervention can reverse a long held market trend. It is more likely that the trend will continue after a short period of price consolidation.

All economic and interest rate reports of the U. S. and Germany are of importance when trading the D-Mark. The results from the G7 meetings can be especially significant.

D-MARK TRADE #1

The June D-Mark Seasonal Chart has a strong downward move from mid-April to June. This represents the movement of investment funds out of the D-Mark and into the U. S. Dollar in anticipation of the seasonal appreciation of the U. S. Treasury Bond (see T-Bond Trade #2). This Mega-Seasonal Trade has had much success, with profits in 15 of the last 18 years traded, for a total profit of $22,478.

PERFORMANCE HISTORY (1977-1997)

Total Profit..$22,478
Total Years Examined 21
Profit Years 15 (83%)
Loss Years 3 (17%)
Inactive Years 3
Average Profit...$1,694
Average Loss $975
Profit-to-Loss Ratio 1.7
Total Profits/Total Losses............................. 8.7

JUNE D-MARK
1977 - 1997

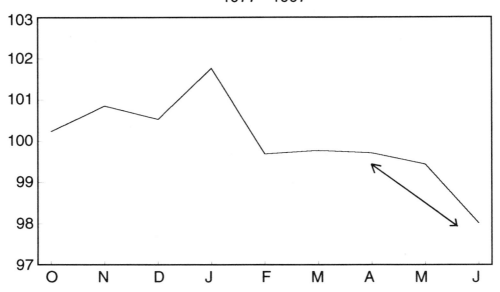

Rules for D-Mark Trade #1:

1. Enters short June D-Mark from April 16th through the first trading day of June.

2. Place a short entry stop 6 ticks below the low of the last 11 trading days. Change this entry stop as needed.

3. When filled, place a protective buy stop 20 ticks above the high of the last 2 trading days.

4. When the high of the last 5 trading days is equal to or below your short entry, lower your stop to 1 tick above the 5 day high. Continue lowering this stop as necessary.

5. Exit this trade on the close of the first trading day after June 11th.

Historical Results for D-Mark Trade #1
June D-Mark

DMM	ENTRY DATE	L/S	PRICE	EXIT DATE	EXIT METHOD	PRICE	TRADE P/L	YEARLY P/L
1977	N/T						$ N/T	$ N/T
1978	04/18/78	S	4899	04/27/78	PSTOP	4862	$ 463	
	05/08/78	S	4809	05/30/78	PSTOP	4749	$ 750	$ 1,213
1979	04/20/79	S	5286	05/30/79	PSTOP	5249	$ 463	$ 463
1980	N/T						$ N/T	$ N/T
1981	04/16/81	S	4593	06/12/81	DATEX	4178	$ 5,188	$ 5,188
1982	05/26/82	S	4304	06/14/82	DATEX	4126	$ 2,225	$ 2,225
1983	04/18/83	S	4101	06/13/83	PSTOP	3929	$ 2,150	$ 2,150
1984	04/18/84	S	3806	05/14/84	PSTOP	3653	$ 1,913	$ 1,913
1985	04/25/85	S	3184	05/09/85	PSTOP	3215	$ (388)	$ (388)
1986	05/06/86	S	4494	06/05/86	PSTOP	4428	$ 825	$ 825
1987	05/26/87	S	5565	06/12/87	DATEX	5523	$ 525	$ 525
1988	05/02/88	S	5968	06/07/88	PSTOP	5845	$ 1,538	$ 1,538
1989	04/28/89	S	5337	05/26/89	PSTOP	5114	$ 2,788	$ 2,788
1990	05/22/90	S	5976	06/12/90	DATEX	5896	$ 1,000	$ 1,000
1991	04/18/91	S	5861	04/30/91	PSTOP	5747	$ 1,425	
	06/03/91	S	5693	06/12/91	DATEX	5584	$ 1,363	$ 2,788
1992	04/16/92	S	5949	05/01/92	PROTS	6048	$ (1,238)	$ (1,238)
1993	05/10/93	S	6215	05/27/93	PSTOP	6189	$ 325	$ 325
1994	N/T						$ N/T	$ N/T
1995	05/11/95	S	7175	05/25/95	PSTOP	6991	$ 2,300	$ 2,300
1996	04/22/96	S	6616	05/07/96	PSTOP	6585	$ 388	
	05/21/96	S	6504	06/12/96	DATEX	6522	$ (225)	$ 163
1997	04/28/97	S	5774	05/09/97	PROTS	5897	$ (1,538)	
	06/02/97	S	5803	06/12/97	DATEX	5784	$ 238	$ (1,300)

TOTAL $ 22,478

Exit Legend:

DATEX = Exit Date
PROTS = Protective Stop
PSTOP = Profit Stop
REV   = Reverse Entry

D-MARK TRADE #2

The September D-Mark Seasonal Chart below indicates a bottoming out of the downward trend in the June/July time period. This is deceptive as you can see from the two directional seasonal charts on the next page. They demonstrate two distinctly different trends after June. *Mega-Seasonals* trades on both sides of this market to profit from the move that develops. Why is there no single direction? It is because the trend is driven from the many government reports issued during June. You cannot be sure which direction the D-Mark will move. Yet, since this trade has shown $52,867 in profits in 17 of the last 21 years, you can be sure that it *will* move!

PERFORMANCE HISTORY (1977-1997)

Total Profit $52,867
Total Years Examined 21
Profit Years 17 (81%)
Loss Years 4 (19%)
Inactive Years 0
Average Profit $3,403
Average Loss $1,250
Profit-to-Loss Ratio 2.7
Total Profits/Total Losses 11.6

SEPTEMBER D-MARK

1977 - 1997

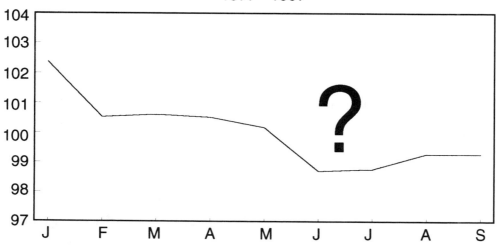

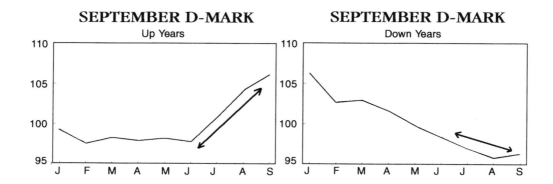

Rules for D-Mark Trade #2

1. Enters September D-Mark futures long and short from the second trading day of June through the first trading day of July.

2. Place a long entry stop 1 tick above the high of the last 21 trading days and a short entry stop 1 tick below the low of the last 21 trading days. Change these as needed.

3. When filled:
   On long: Place a protective sell stop 1 tick below the 4 day low.
   On short: Place a protective buy stop 1 tick above the 4 day high.

   Remember to continue entering the opposite entry as described in #2, until you are no longer in the trade entry window. Should you already have entered a trade via #2 and the reverse entry price is greater than your protective sell stop or profit stop (for longs) use the entry price to exit the current trade so that your new position is short. Of course, should you presently be short, adjust the protective buy stop or profit stop.

4. If long: When the low of the last 10 trading days is equal to or greater than the entry price, raise your stop to 1 point below the 10 day low.
   If short: When the high of the last 10 trading days is equal to or less than the entry price, lower your stop to 1 point over the 10 day high.
   Continue changing the stop as necessary.

5. Exit long trade on the close of the first trading day after August 22nd. Exit short trade on the close of the first trading day after August 9th.

Historical Results for D-Mark Trade #2
September D-Mark

DMU	ENTRY DATE	L/S	PRICE	EXIT DATE	EXIT METHOD	PRICE	TRADE P/L	YEARLY P/L
1977	06/24/77	L	4283	07/28/77	PSTOP	4389	$ 1,325	$ 1,325
1978	06/28/78	L	4891	08/21/78	PSTOP	4988	$ 1,213	$ 1,213
1979	06/15/79	L	5343	07/06/79	PSTOP	5434	$ 1,138	$ 1,138
1980	06/13/80	L	5700	06/16/80	PROTS	5652	$ (600)	$ (600)
1981	06/02/81	S	4274	08/10/81	DATEX	3908	$ 4,575	$ 4,575
1982	06/02/82	S	4265	07/20/82	PSTOP	4109	$ 1,950	$ 1,950
1983	06/06/83	S	3940	08/10/83	DATEX	3686	$ 3,175	$ 3,175
1984	06/04/84	L	3807	06/15/84	PROTS	3705	$ (1,275)	
	06/19/84	S	3664	08/10/84	DATEX	3459	$ 2,563	$ 1,288
1985	06/18/85	L	3341	08/23/85	DATEX	3644	$ 3,788	$ 3,788
1986	07/01/86	L	4603	08/25/86	DATEX	4903	$ 3,750	$ 3,750
1987	06/22/87	S	5492	06/24/87	PROTS	5542	$ (625)	$ (625)
1988	06/02/88	S	5837	08/10/88	DATEX	5255	$ 7,275	$ 7,275
1989	06/12/89	S	4949	06/22/89	PROTS	5140	$ (2,388)	
	06/23/89	L	5198	08/07/89	PSTOP	5239	$ 513	$ (1,875)
1990	06/04/90	S	5874	06/19/90	PROTS	5993	$ (1,488)	
	06/26/90	L	5996	08/23/90	DATEX	6475	$ 5,988	$ 4,500
1991	06/07/91	S	5641	07/12/91	PSTOP	5558	$ 1,038	$ 1,038
1992	06/05/92	L	6185	08/24/92	DATEX	7103	$ 11,475	$ 11,475
1993	06/15/93	S	6014	07/20/93	PSTOP	5853	$ 2,013	$ 2,013
1994	06/15/94	L	6093	07/21/94	PSTOP	6314	$ 2,763	$ 2,763
1995	06/29/95	L	7271	07/12/95	PROTS	7119	$ (1,900)	$ (1,900)
1996	06/14/96	L	6626	08/15/96	PSTOP	6725	$ 1,238	$ 1,238
1997	06/04/97	S	5814	08/11/97	DATEX	5385	$ 5,363	$ 5,363

TOTAL $ 52,867

Exit Legend:

DATEX = Exit Date
PROTS = Protective Stop
PSTOP = Profit Stop
REV   = Reverse Entry

D-MARK TRADE #3

The D-Mark Trade #3 positions itself to take advantage of the year-end "book squaring" in Germany. The March D-Mark Seasonal Chart reveals the result, a large downward move into the February time period. Mega-Seasonals D-Mark Trade #3 profits from this trend, earning $31,728 since 1977.

PERFORMANCE HISTORY (1977-1998)

Total Profit $31,728
Total Years Examined 22
Profit Years 16 (89%)
Loss Years 2 (11%)
Inactive Years 4
Average Profit $2,152
Average Loss $1,350
Profit-to-Loss Ratio 1.6
Total Profits/Total Losses 12.8

MARCH D-MARK

1977 - 1998

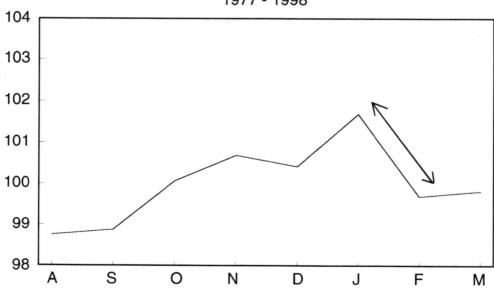

Rules for D-Mark Trade #3:

1. Enters short March D-Mark from the second trading day of November through the last trading day of January.

2. Place a short entry stop 2 ticks below the low of the last 22 trading days. Move this entry stop as necessary.

3. When filled, place a protective buy stop 1 tick above the high of the last 4 trading days.

4. When the high of the last 9 trading days is equal to or less than your entry price, lower your stop to 1 tick above the 9-day high. Continue lowering this as necessary.

5. Exit trade on the close of the first trading day after March 7th.

Historical Results for D-Mark Trade #3
March D-Mark

DMH	ENTRY DATE	L/S	PRICE	EXIT DATE	EXIT METHOD	PRICE	TRADE P/L	YEARLY P/L
1977	01/18/77	S	4164	02/11/77	PSTOP	4163	$ 13	$ 13
1978	N/T						$ N/T	$ N/T
1979	11/16/78	S	5378	12/11/78	PSTOP	5371	$ 88	
	01/25/79	S	5425	03/08/79	DATEX	5404	$ 263	$ 351
1980	01/22/80	S	5808	03/10/80	DATEX	5531	$ 3,463	$ 3,463
1981	11/05/80	S	5278	11/11/80	PROTS	5423	$ (1,813)	
	12/05/80	S	5223	02/20/81	PSTOP	4812	$ 5,138	$ 3,325
1982	12/11/81	S	4437	03/08/82	PSTOP	4277	$ 2,000	$ 2,000
1983	11/03/82	S	3934	11/19/82	PROTS	3974	$ (500)	
	01/19/83	S	4156	02/10/83	PSTOP	4158	$ (25)	$ (525)
1984	11/03/83	S	3818	12/27/83	PSTOP	3672	$ 1,825	
	01/04/84	S	3607	02/02/84	PSTOP	3637	$ (375)	$ 1,450
1985	11/26/84	S	3305	03/08/85	DATEX	2939	$ 4,575	$ 4,575
1986	N/T						$ N/T	$ N/T
1987	N/T						$ N/T	$ N/T
1988	01/15/88	S	6063	02/26/88	PSTOP	5933	$ 1,625	$ 1,625
1989	12/20/88	S	5677	02/10/89	PSTOP	5445	$ 2,900	$ 2,900
1990	N/T						$ N/T	$ N/T
1991	12/21/90	S	6570	01/31/91	PSTOP	6744	$ (2,175)	$ (2,175)
1992	01/15/92	S	6127	03/02/92	PSTOP	6116	$ 138	$ 138
1993	11/04/92	S	6245	01/14/93	PSTOP	6119	$ 1,575	$ 1,575
1994	11/02/93	S	5826	01/27/94	PSTOP	5744	$ 1,025	$ 1,025
1995	11/14/94	S	6486	12/28/94	PSTOP	6388	$ 1,225	$ 1,225
1996	11/27/95	S	7053	02/05/96	PSTOP	6816	$ 2,963	$ 2,963
1997	11/25/96	S	6615	12/31/96	PSTOP	6523	$ 1,150	
	01/03/97	S	6415	02/26/97	PSTOP	5997	$ 5,225	$ 6,375
1998	11/27/97	S	5698	12/31/97	OPEN	5584	$ 1,425	$ 1,425

TOTAL $ 31,728

Exit Legend:

DATEX = Exit Date
PROTS = Protective Stop
PSTOP = Profit Stop
REV   = Reverse Entry

- Chapter 12 -

GOLD

The COMEX Division of the New York Mercantile Exchange began trading Gold futures in 1974, and options on those futures in 1982. Previous to that time, it had been illegal for individuals in the U. S. to own gold, except in the form of jewelry and antique coins. Gold is often called the "Yellow Metal." South Africa is the world's largest producer of gold.

It has been said that every ounce of gold ever discovered is still around somewhere. This is a useful fact to keep in mind when it comes to understanding the supply side of the supply/demand equation. The supply of gold is totally price dependent. As the price of gold rises, not only do old and new mines start filling the demand need, but scrap gold seems to pour into the market from everywhere. This keeps a lid on any major price increase.

Since price controls supply, what controls demand? Jewelry and electronic equipment manufacturing (including computers) play a large role in the demand for gold. But another worldwide use for gold, as a safe haven or storage of value, is just as important. A political upheaval can have a major effect on gold's price. In various parts of the world gold is a far safer investment than currency.

Reports a gold trader should watch are the same economic reports that affect currencies, the economy and interest rates. Reports such as the Unemployment Reports, Producer and Consumer Price Indexes, Balance of Trade and even Housing Starts affect the price of gold.

GOLD TRADE #1

Year-end book-squaring by central banks, sales of surplus gold from mining companies and realignment of investment objectives drives down the price of June gold from January through May. The June Gold Seasonal Chart shows this quite well. Mega-Seasonals Gold Trade #1 has an excellent 22 year success rate netting $64,480 in profits and trading every year.

PERFORMANCE HISTORY (1977-1998)

Total Profit	$64,480
Total Years Examined	22
Profit Years	17 (77%)
Loss Years	5 (23%)
Inactive Years	0
Average Profit	$4,016
Average Loss	$758
Profit-to-Loss Ratio	5.3
Total Profits/Total Losses	18.0

JUNE GOLD
1977 - 1998

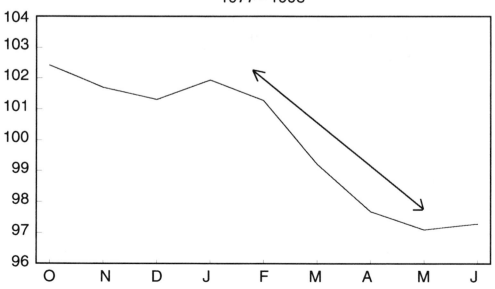

Rules for Gold Trade #1:

1. Enters short June (COMEX) Gold from the first trading day of December through the last trading day of March.

2. Place a short entry stop 1 tick under the low of the last 17 trading days. Move this entry stop as necessary.

3. When filled, place a protective buy stop 1 tick above the high of the last 3 trading days.

4. When the high of the last 13 trading days is equal to or less than the entry price, lower your stop to 1 tick above the 13 day high. Move this stop when needed.

5. Exit trade on the close of the first trading day after May 5th.

Historical Results for Gold Trade #1
June COMEX Gold

GCM	ENTRY DATE	L/S	PRICE	EXIT DATE	EXIT METHOD	PRICE	TRADE P/L	YEARLY P/L
1977	01/10/77	S	133.30	02/07/77	PROTS	137.20	$ (390)	$ (390)
1978	02/09/78	S	176.40	02/10/78	PROTS	180.20	$ (380)	$
	03/20/78	S	183.30	05/08/78	DATEX	172.60	$ 1,070	$ 690
1979	03/05/79	S	244.50	05/07/79	DATEX	251.70	$ (720)	$ (720)
1980	02/25/80	S	653.40	05/06/80	DATEX	510.00	$ 14,340	$ 14,340
1981	12/09/80	S	654.00	03/17/81	PSTOP	515.60	$ 13,840	$ 13,840
1982	12/22/81	S	419.90	04/05/82	PSTOP	343.50	$ 7,640	$ 7,640
1983	02/22/83	S	502.40	04/05/83	PSTOP	434.60	$ 6,780	$ 6,780
1984	12/16/83	S	393.90	02/01/84	PSTOP	390.60	$ 330	
	03/16/84	S	399.90	05/07/84	DATEX	374.50	$ 2,540	$ 2,870
1985	12/07/84	S	340.10	03/18/85	PSTOP	302.10	$ 3,800	$ 3,800
1986	12/02/85	S	334.90	01/09/86	PROTS	345.30	$ (1,040)	
	02/04/86	S	346.50	05/06/86	DATEX	344.00	$ 250	$ (790)
1987	01/30/87	S	407.40	03/27/87	PROTS	425.60	$ (1,820)	$ (1,820)
1988	01/15/88	S	488.90	03/15/88	PSTOP	450.30	$ 3,860	$ 3,860
1989	12/15/88	S	431.10	03/08/89	PSTOP	401.60	$ 2,950	
	03/28/89	S	390.90	05/08/89	DATEX	378.40	$ 1,250	$ 4,200
1990	12/27/89	S	415.70	01/12/90	PROTS	428.00	$ (1,230)	
	02/26/90	S	419.90	05/07/90	DATEX	374.00	$ 4,590	$ 3,360
1991	12/03/90	S	386.80	12/28/90	PROTS	399.60	$ (1,280)	
	01/17/91	S	385.90	03/06/91	PSTOP	375.10	$ 1,080	
	03/25/91	S	363.20	05/06/91	DATEX	356.90	$ 630	$ 430
1992	12/12/91	S	367.90	01/20/92	PSTOP	363.30	$ 460	
	02/18/92	S	356.00	05/06/92	DATEX	337.50	$ 1,850	$ 2,310
1993	12/21/92	S	336.60	01/29/93	PSTOP	333.20	$ 340	
	02/26/93	S	329.40	03/19/93	PROTS	333.50	$ (410)	$ (70)
1994	01/10/94	S	387.00	03/10/94	PSTOP	385.70	$ 130	$ 130
1995	12/01/94	S	391.40	02/17/95	PSTOP	383.60	$ 780	
	03/01/95	S	379.40	03/07/95	PROTS	385.20	$ (580)	$ 200
1996	02/20/96	S	404.40	03/26/96	PSTOP	402.60	$ 180	$ 180
1997	12/02/96	S	377.30	02/20/97	PSTOP	351.60	$ 2,570	
	03/18/97	S	349.90	05/06/97	DATEX	341.50	$ 840	$ 3,410
1998	12/01/97	S	300.40	12/23/97	PSTOP	298.10	$ 230	$ 230

TOTAL $ 64,480

Exit Legend:

DATEX = Exit Date
PROTS = Protective Stop
PSTOP = Profit Stop
REV   = Reverse Entry

- Chapter 13 -

HEATING OIL

Heating Oil futures were the first petroleum futures contract to be traded. The New York Mercantile Exchange began trading Heating Oil in 1978. The size of a heating oil contract is 42,000 gallons. Options on heating oil futures have been traded since 1987. Heating Oil is second only to gasoline in the "cut" from a barrel of oil.

The supply of heating oil is determined by the refineries' production. During the fall and winter periods the refineries concentrate production on heating oil. In early spring heating oil inventories are normally at a low point. An extremely cold winter, especially in the Northeastern United States, where the use of heating oil is greatest, can deplete these supplies. When this happens, it is not unusual for prices to rally with unequalled ferocity.

Heating oil demand is very inelastic. It can be extremely costly and time consuming to convert commercial and home heating plants over to burn other suitable fuels.

The main report to keep an eye on is the weekly American Petroleum Institute's (API) Stocks Report when trading heating oil futures.

HEATING OIL TRADE #1

Heating Oil Trade #1 takes advantage of the March reaction to the long-term downtrend starting in November. Winter is on the wane, refineries are beginning to concentrate on gasoline production and the supply of heating oil declines. The perfect time for an upward trend to develop. And so it does, with amazing regularity. Mega-Seasonals Heating Oil Trade #1 has traded all but one of the last sixteen years for a profit of $26,391. Be sure to follow this trade every year. The stats are excellent!

PERFORMANCE HISTORY (1982-1997)

Total Profit..$26,391
Total Years Examined 16
Profit Years 12 (80%)
Loss Years 3 (20%)
Inactive Years 1
Average Profit...$2,362
Average Loss $652
Profit-to-Loss Ratio 3.6
Total Profits/Total Losses...........................14.5

MAY HEATING OIL
1982 - 1997

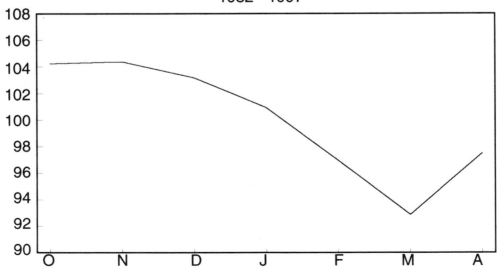

Rules for Heating Oil Trade #1:

1. Enters long May Heating Oil from the first trading day of March through the 2nd trading day of April.

2. Place a long entry stop 1 tick above the high of the last 16 trading days. As this high drops, move your entry stop lower.

3. When filled, place a protective sell stop 1 tick below the low of the last 3 trading days.

4. When the low of the last 9 trading days is equal to or greater than your entry, raise your stop to 1 tick below the low of the last 9 trading days. Move this stop as the low of the last 9 days increases.

5. Exit this trade on the close of the first trading day after April 23rd.

Historical Results for Heating Oil Trade #1
May Heating Oil

HOK	ENTRY DATE	L/S	PRICE	EXIT DATE	EXIT METHOD	PRICE	TRADE P/L	YEARLY P/L
1982	03/25/82	L	7375	04/26/82	DATEX	9274	$ 7,976	$ 7,976
1983	03/15/83	L	7211	04/25/83	DATEX	8454	$ 5,221	$ 5,221
1984	03/28/84	L	7960	04/24/84	DATEX	8375	$ 1,743	$ 1,743
1985	03/04/85	L	7031	04/11/85	PSTOP	7499	$ 1,966	$ 1,966
1986	N/T						$ N/T	$ N/T
1987	03/09/87	L	4885	04/24/87	DATEX	4960	$ 315	$ 315
1988	03/18/88	L	4331	04/25/88	DATEX	5121	$ 3,318	$ 3,318
1989	03/02/89	L	4936	04/05/89	PSTOP	5229	$ 1,231	$ 1,231
1990	04/02/90	L	5491	04/10/90	PROTS	5299	$ (806)	$ (806)
1991	03/20/91	L	5551	04/24/91	DATEX	5647	$ 403	$ 403
1992	03/13/92	L	5250	04/23/92	DATEX	5489	$ 1,004	$ 1,004
1993	03/04/93	L	5781	03/11/93	PROTS	5664	$ (491)	$ (491)
1994	04/04/94	L	4446	04/25/94	DATEX	4823	$ 1,583	$ 1,583
1995	03/27/95	L	4771	04/24/95	DATEX	5002	$ 970	$ 970
1996	03/13/96	L	5176	04/17/96	PSTOP	5799	$ 2,617	$ 2,617
1997	03/18/97	L	5581	03/31/97	PROTS	5424	$ (659)	$ (659)

TOTAL $ 26,391

Exit Legend:

DATEX = Exit Date
PROTS = Protective Stop
PSTOP = Profit Stop
REV   = Reverse Entry

HEATING OIL TRADE #2

Heating oil inventories are low in the July/August time period. Orders from heating oil suppliers are starting to build up. This causes a supply shortage that refineries need to fill. This also gives Mega-Seasonals Heating Oil Trade #2 a nice profit of $41,049 in the last 18 years. The November Heating Oil Seasonal Chart shows this distinct up trend from July through October.

PERFORMANCE HISTORY (1980-1997)

Total Profit	$41,049
Total Years Examined	18
Profit Years	14 (78%)
Loss Years	4 (22%)
Inactive Years	0
Average Profit	$3,259
Average Loss	$1,145
Profit-to-Loss Ratio	2.8
Total Profits/Total Losses	10.0

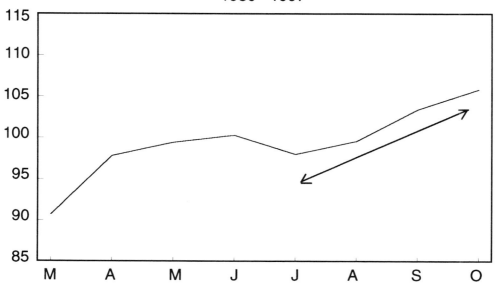

NOVEMBER HEATING OIL
1980 - 1997

Rules for Heating Oil Trade #2:

1. Enters long November Heating Oil from the first trading day of July through the last trading day of September.

2. Place a buy stop 1 tick above the high of the last 19 trading days. Lower this entry stop as necessary.

3. When filled place a protective sell stop 1 tick below the low of the last 5 trading days.

4. When the low of the last 11 trading days is equal to or greater than your entry, raise your stop to 1 tick below the 11 day low. Raise this as needed.

5. Exit this trade on the close of the first trading day after October 11th.

Historical Results for Heating Oil Trade #2
November Heating Oil

HOX	ENTRY DATE	L/S	PRICE	EXIT DATE	EXIT METHOD	PRICE	TRADE P/L	YEARLY P/L
1980	09/03/80	L	7891	10/13/80	DATEX	8125	$ 983	$ 983
1981	07/06/81	L	9681	08/10/81	PSTOP	9778	$ 407	
	08/20/81	L	9960	08/21/81	PROTS	9774	$ (781)	
	09/24/81	L	9651	10/12/81	DATEX	9790	$ 584	$ 210
1982	08/09/82	L	9181	10/12/82	DATEX	10100	$ 3,860	$ 3,860
1983	07/13/83	L	8601	08/22/83	PSTOP	8669	$ 286	$ 286
1984	08/17/84	L	8026	10/04/84	PSTOP	8219	$ 811	$ 811
1985	07/10/85	L	7121	09/13/85	PSTOP	7719	$ 2,512	
	09/23/85	L	8026	10/10/85	DATEX	8089	$ 265	$ 2,777
1986	08/05/86	L	4063	09/08/86	PSTOP	4474	$ 1,726	$ 1,726
1987	07/09/87	L	5695	07/24/87	PROTS	5579	$ (487)	
	09/15/87	L	5380	10/12/87	DATEX	5580	$ 840	$ 353
1988	07/20/88	L	4681	09/06/88	PROTS	4239	$ (1,856)	$ (1,856)
1989	07/18/89	L	5306	07/28/89	PROTS	5059	$ (1,037)	
	08/21/89	L	5301	10/12/89	DATEX	6117	$ 3,427	$ 2,390
1990	07/12/90	L	5395	10/12/90	DATEX	10536	$ 21,592	$ 21,592
1991	07/02/91	L	5966	08/07/91	PSTOP	6074	$ 454	
	08/16/91	L	6276	09/09/91	PSTOP	6275	$ (4)	
	09/24/91	L	6586	10/14/91	DATEX	6908	$ 1,352	$ 1,802
1992	08/31/92	L	6201	10/12/92	DATEX	6548	$ 1,457	$ 1,457
1993	08/12/93	L	5485	09/10/93	PROTS	5164	$ (1,348)	
	09/29/93	L	5531	10/12/93	DATEX	5622	$ 382	$ (966)
1994	07/29/94	L	5431	08/05/94	PROTS	5237	$ (815)	$ (815)
1995	08/01/95	L	5046	09/20/95	PSTOP	5154	$ 454	$ 454
1996	07/01/96	L	5526	07/26/96	PSTOP	5639	$ 475	
	08/02/96	L	5871	10/14/96	DATEX	7407	$ 6,451	$ 6,926
1997	07/02/97	L	5701	07/10/97	PROTS	5453	$ (1,042)	
	07/30/97	L	5716	08/25/97	PROTS	5494	$ (932)	
	09/22/97	L	5581	10/13/97	DATEX	5827	$ 1,033	$ (941)

TOTAL $ 41,049

Exit Legend:

DATEX = Exit Date
PROTS = Protective Stop
PSTOP = Profit Stop
REV   = Reverse Entry

HEATING OIL TRADE #3

Mega-Seasonals Heating Oil Trade #3 profits from the strong seasonal downtrend from November through March. The April Heating Oil Seasonal Chart shows this quite well. But why, during the winter, would heating oil prices decline? First, the refineries are in full heating oil production and have built up an inventory. Second, heating oil distributors have placed their orders well in advance, much as toy stores place their Christmas orders in July. Barring a surprisingly extreme winter in the Northeast, all of the unknowns are now known. So prices decline. Total profits for this trade have been $37,923 over the last 18 trading years.

PERFORMANCE HISTORY (1981-1998)

Total Profit $37,923
Total Years Examined 18
Profit Years 12 (67%)
Loss Years 6 (33%)
Inactive Years 0
Average Profit $3,739
Average Loss $1,157
Profit-to-Loss Ratio 3.2
Total Profits/Total Losses 6.5

APRIL HEATING OIL
1981 - 1998

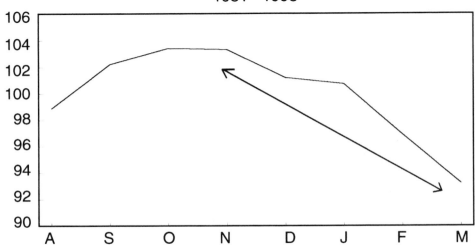

Rules for Heating Oil Trade #3:

1. Enters short April Heating Oil from the first trading day of November through January 16th.

2. Place a short entry stop 1 tick below the low of the last 10 trading days. Move this entry stop as the 10 day low rises.

3. When filled, place a protective buy stop 1 tick above the high of the last 5 trading days.

4. When the high of the last 10 days is equal to or less than your entry price, lower the stop to 1 tick above the 10 day high.

5. Exit this trade on the close of the first trading day of March.

Historical Results for Heating Oil Trade #3
April Heating Oil

HOJ	ENTRY DATE	L/S	PRICE	EXIT DATE	EXIT METHOD	PRICE	TRADE P/L	YEARLY P/L
1981	12/08/80	S	9899	01/06/81	PSTOP	10600	$ (2,944)	$ (2,944)
1982	11/16/81	S	10084	03/01/82	DATEX	7769	$ 9,723	$ 9,723
1983	11/11/82	S	9095	12/09/82	PSTOP	8470	$ 2,625	
	12/22/82	S	7939	03/01/83	DATEX	7236	$ 2,953	$ 5,578
1984	11/11/83	S	7749	12/21/83	PSTOP	7580	$ 710	
	01/06/84	S	7379	01/16/84	PROTS	7815	$ (1,831)	$ (1,121)
1985	11/19/84	S	7259	01/31/85	PSTOP	6851	$ 1,714	$ 1,714
1986	11/27/85	S	7689	12/27/85	PSTOP	7046	$ 2,701	
	01/09/86	S	6574	03/03/86	DATEX	4172	$ 10,088	$ 12,789
1987	11/20/86	S	4214	12/12/86	PROTS	4420	$ (865)	$ (865)
1988	11/04/87	S	5120	12/30/87	PSTOP	4660	$ 1,932	
	01/12/88	S	4430	03/01/88	DATEX	4347	$ 349	$ 2,281
1989	11/17/88	S	3829	11/23/88	PROTS	4000	$ (718)	$ (718)
1990	11/14/89	S	5250	11/24/89	PROTS	5421	$ (718)	
	01/08/90	S	5579	03/01/90	DATEX	5463	$ 487	$ (231)
1991	11/16/90	S	7390	12/26/90	PSTOP	6951	$ 1,844	
	01/03/91	S	6529	01/09/91	PROTS	7221	$ (2,906)	$ (1,062)
1992	11/11/91	S	6104	01/13/92	PSTOP	5366	$ 3,100	$ 3,100
1993	11/04/92	S	5699	12/16/92	PSTOP	5536	$ 685	
	01/04/93	S	5459	01/25/93	PSTOP	5456	$ 13	$ 698
1994	11/08/93	S	5124	01/05/94	PSTOP	4576	$ 2,302	$ 2,302
1995	11/14/94	S	4954	12/27/94	PSTOP	4916	$ 160	
	01/10/95	S	4839	03/01/95	DATEX	4644	$ 819	$ 979
1996	01/11/96	S	5189	02/01/96	PSTOP	5051	$ 580	$ 580
1997	11/05/96	S	5949	11/13/96	PROTS	6251	$ (1,268)	
	11/26/96	S	6114	12/02/96	PROTS	6401	$ (1,205)	
	01/15/97	S	6469	03/03/97	DATEX	5318	$ 4,834	$ 2,361
1998	11/05/97	S	5644	12/31/97	OPEN	4987	$ 2,759	$ 2,759

TOTAL $ 37,923

Exit Legend:

DATEX = Exit Date
PROTS = Protective Stop
 PSTOP = Profit Stop
 REV   = Reverse Entry

- Chapter 14 -

LIVE HOGS

The Chicago Mercantile Exchange began trading Live Hog futures in 1966. In 1995, the Live Hog Contract was revised to cash settlement and renamed "Lean Hogs." A contract of Lean Hogs is 40,000 lbs. Options are traded on Lean Hog futures. The MidAmerica Commodity Exchange trades a 25,000 lbs. contract of Hogs.

Half of all hog production is in the four main Corn Belt states of Iowa, Illinois, Indiana and Missouri. The price of hogs is influenced more by supply than demand. The inventory of marketable hogs depends on decisions made by hog producers ten months earlier, using the market conditions and prices at that time. The size of the pig crop and the pattern of hog slaughter is a reflection of the price of feed corn. If the price of feed corn is relatively high it is more profitable to sell the corn than to feed it to hogs. Alternately, should the price of corn be low, feeding it to hogs can be more profitable and cost effective.

The demand for hogs is very elastic depending on the relative price of food substitutes such as beef, poultry, lamb and fish. The higher the relative price of pork, the lower the demand.

Two reports that must be watched carefully when trading hogs are the Hog and Pig Report (released quarterly in March, June, September and December) and the Cold Storage Report (issued monthly). It is rare when the hog and pork belly markets don't react fiercely to any surprises contained in these reports.

LIVE HOG TRADE #1

A late February Cold Storage Report revealing lower belly inventories often combines with a bullish Hogs and Pigs Report (issued in late March) to ignite the long term uptrend in June Live Hogs. The June Live Hog Seasonal Chart shows how this develops. In the last 21 years, this trade has earned $24,170 by being profitable 88% of the years traded.

PERFORMANCE HISTORY (1977-1997)

Total Profit $24,170
Total Years Examined 21
Profit Years 14 (88%)
Loss Years 2 (12%)
Inactive Years 5
Average Profit $1,810
Average Loss $585
Profit-to-Loss Ratio 3.1
Total Profits/Total Losses 21.7

JUNE LIVE HOGS
1977 - 1997

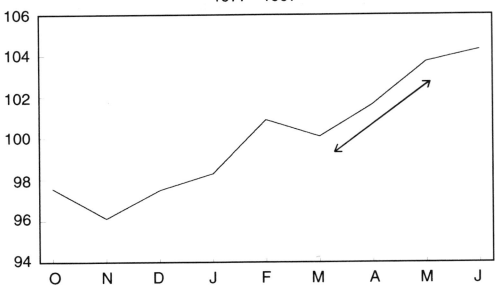

Rules for Live Hog Trade #1:

1. Enters long June Live Hogs from the first trading day of March through the first trading day of May.

2. Place a long entry stop 1 tick (2 1/2 points) above the high of the last 21 trading days. Lower this entry as needed.

3. When filled, place a protective stop 1 tick (2 1/2 points) below the low of the last 5 trading days.

4. When the low of the last 15 trading days is equal to or greater than the entry price, move your stop to 1 tick under the 15 day low. Move this stop when necessary.

5. Exit trade on the close of the first trading day after May 27th.

Historical Results for Live Hog Trade #1
June Live Hogs

LHM	ENTRY DATE	L/S	PRICE	EXIT DATE	EXIT METHOD	PRICE	TRADE P/L	YEARLY P/L
1977	03/15/77	L	39.075	05/31/77	DATEX	45.000	$ 2,370	$ 2,370
1978	03/08/78	L	49.850	05/30/78	DATEX	54.075	$ 1,690	$ 1,690
1979	N/T						$ N/T	$ N/T
1980	N/T						$ N/T	$ N/T
1981	03/31/81	L	49.675	05/28/81	DATEX	51.750	$ 830	$ 830
1982	03/04/82	L	53.075	05/28/82	DATEX	62.125	$ 3,620	$ 3,620
1983	N/T						$ N/T	$ N/T
1984	03/05/84	L	53.225	04/25/84	PSTOP	55.275	$ 820	$ 820
1985	N/T						$ N/T	$ N/T
1986	03/12/86	L	44.775	04/04/86	PROTS	42.400	$ (950)	
	04/29/86	L	44.925	05/28/86	DATEX	50.050	$ 2,050	$ 1,100
1987	03/13/87	L	47.175	05/28/87	DATEX	58.150	$ 4,390	$ 4,390
1988	03/17/88	L	49.475	05/31/88	DATEX	54.775	$ 2,120	$ 2,120
1989	03/01/89	L	48.700	03/20/89	PROTS	47.525	$ (470)	$ (470)
1990	03/06/90	L	55.125	05/29/90	DATEX	67.250	$ 4,850	$ 4,850
1991	03/01/91	L	57.425	05/28/91	DATEX	57.650	$ 90	$ 90
1992	04/03/92	L	46.800	05/18/92	PSTOP	47.050	$ 100	$ 100
1993	03/02/93	L	51.325	04/06/93	PSTOP	53.400	$ 830	$ 830
1994	N/T						$ N/T	$ N/T
1995	03/02/95	L	46.125	03/24/95	PROTS	44.375	$ (700)	$ (700)
1996	03/05/96	L	53.825	04/26/96	PSTOP	55.800	$ 790	
	05/01/96	L	59.975	05/28/96	DATEX	62.650	$ 1,070	$ 1,860
1997	03/24/97	L	81.000	05/15/97	PSTOP	82.675	$ 670	$ 670

TOTAL $ 24,170

Exit Legend:

DATEX = Exit Date
PROTS = Protective Stop
PSTOP = Profit Stop
REV   = Reverse Entry

- Chapter 15 -

LUMBER

Futures on Lumber began trading on the Chicago Mercantile Exchange in 1972. In 1996, the size of the contract was decreased to 80,000 board feet to encourage greater trading volume. Options on the futures contract are also traded. Lumber futures can be somewhat of a thin market, but it is tradeable.

Strikes and weather conditions in Washington, Oregon and Northern California (where 75% of lumber is grown), can have a tremendous influence on the available supply of lumber. Government Forestry Management Programs and Species Preservation Programs have often had a devastating effect on lumber production.

Demand for lumber has been increasing rapidly, due to exports and new home construction. The seasonal demand for lumber is highest during the summer months, the main building season. Interest rates, the general direction of interest rates, general economic conditions and even the stock market's behavior encourage new home construction.

The Housing Starts Report is a most valuable report when trading the lumber market. This report is a prime mover in the price of lumber.

LUMBER TRADE #1

During the first quarter of the year lumber prices follow the direction of interest rate futures downward. As T-Bond futures drop, mortgage rates rise and projected new housing expectations fall. Lower housing starts equals less demand for lumber and lower lumber prices. This trend is revealed in the July Lumber Seasonal Chart. The decline begins in March and ends in the May/July time period. This trade has shown a profit of $32,760, based on the new contract size of 80,000 board feet.

PERFORMANCE HISTORY (1977-1997)

Total Profit..$32,760
Total Years Examined 21
Profit Years 15 (75%)
Loss Years 5 (25%)
Inactive Years 1
Average Profit...$2,353
Average Loss $507
Profit-to-Loss Ratio 4.6
Total Profits/Total Losses...........................13.9

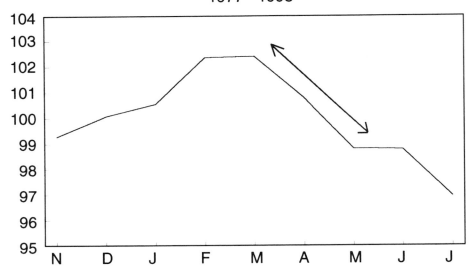

JULY LUMBER
1977 - 1998

Rules for Lumber Trade #1:

1. Enters short July Lumber from the first trading day of February through the last trading day of March.

2. Place a short entry stop 3 ticks below the low of the last 10 trading days. Raise this stop as the 10 day low moves higher.

3. When filled place a protective buy stop 2 ticks above the high of the last 4 trading days.

4. When the high of the last 11 trading days is equal to or less than the entry price, lower your stop to 1 tick above the 11 day high. As the 11 day high decreases, lower this stop.

5. Exit trade on the close of the first trading day after May 27th.

Historical Results for Lumber Trade #1
July Lumber (160,000 board feet unless otherwise noted)

LBN	ENTRY DATE	L/S	PRICE	EXIT DATE	EXIT METHOD	PRICE	TRADE P/L	YEARLY P/L
1977	03/08/77	S	200.10	03/17/77	PROTS	207.20	$ (1,136)	
	03/29/77	S	196.20	05/31/77	DATEX	180.40	$ 2,528	$ 1,392
1978	02/23/78	S	209.70	04/24/78	PSTOP	202.90	$ 1,088	$ 1,088
1979	03/06/79	S	217.70	04/16/79	PSTOP	214.10	$ 576	$ 576
1980	02/06/80	S	231.20	02/14/80	PROTS	242.00	$ (1,728)	
	02/20/80	S	228.60	04/21/80	PSTOP	179.50	$ 7,856	$ 6,128
1981	02/10/81	S	200.00	03/13/81	PSTOP	195.00	$ 800	
	03/27/81	S	187.50	04/09/81	PROTS	196.40	$ (1,424)	$ (624)
1982	02/02/82	S	157.90	03/17/82	PSTOP	156.90	$ 160	$ 160
1983	02/08/83	S	205.00	04/11/83	PSTOP	203.60	$ 224	$ 224
1984	02/10/84	S	195.20	02/29/84	PROTS	202.80	$ (1,216)	
	03/27/84	S	202.40	05/29/84	DATEX	144.00	$ 9,344	$ 8,128
1985	02/01/85	S	165.50	04/04/85	PSTOP	140.30	$ 4,032	$ 4,032
1986	02/04/86	S	146.80	02/14/86	PROTS	151.80	$ (800)	
	03/26/86	S	176.30	05/28/86	DATEX	171.90	$ 704	$ (96)
1987	02/19/87	S	176.10	03/17/87	PROTS	183.10	$ (1,120)	
	03/31/87	S	180.30	05/28/87	DATEX	179.60	$ 112	$ (1,008)
1988	02/24/88	S	188.00	03/14/88	PSTOP	187.00	$ 160	$ 160
1989	02/24/89	S	189.70	03/29/89	PSTOP	188.00	$ 272	$ 272
1990	02/23/90	S	200.50	03/20/90	PSTOP	197.80	$ 432	$ 432
1991	N/T						$ N/T	$ N/T
1992	02/11/92	S	234.10	02/21/92	PROTS	242.80	$ (1,392)	
	03/26/92	S	242.70	05/14/92	PSTOP	236.80	$ 944	$ (448)
1993	03/24/93	S	411.00	05/28/93	DATEX	266.00	$ 23,200	$ 23,200
1994	03/09/94	S	437.10	05/05/94	PSTOP	369.30	$ 10,848	$ 10,848
1995	02/17/95	S	330.00	05/30/95	DATEX	246.50	$ 13,360	$ 13,360
1996	02/20/96	S	306.00	04/17/96	PROTS	324.10	$ (2,896)	$ (2,896)
1997	02/26/97	S	378.70	04/01/97	PSTOP	375.00	$ 296	$ 296 *

TOTAL $ 65,224

* 80,000 board feet

Exit Legend:

DATEX = Exit Date
PROTS = Protective Stop
PSTOP = Profit Stop
REV   = Reverse Entry

- Chapter 16 -

NEW YORK STOCK EXCHANGE INDEX (NYSE)

Futures on the NYSE Index began trading on the FINEX Exchange in 1982, with options on these futures following in 1983. It is valued at $500 times the index number. The NYSE is a numeric representation of the value of the stocks traded on the NYSE.

Like other stock indices, the NYSE Stock Index is a demand driven market. The demand side of this market is determined by how individual and institutional investors feel about the future of the economy and the future of the overall stock market. Economic statistics and reports, housing starts, and interest rates are only a few of the many factors that influence this market. Should the majority of investors feel positive about the economy, the stock market indices will rise. On the other hand, should investors feel undecided or negative the markets will drop.

When trading the NYSE Index it is important to watch all the economic reports issued for any dramatic changes. There are literally dozens of reports released each month. It is also very important to watch the interest rate markets. Normally, both stocks and interest rate markets trend together. Remember, that when interest rate markets are rising the actual interest rate yield is declining. This decreases the cost of borrowing and increases corporate profits.

NYSE INDEX TRADE #1

Mega-Seasonals NYSE Index Trade #1 has been designed to profit from the seasonal increase in the equity markets from May to June. This is known as the summer rally. Money invested in various interest rate vehicles is transferred into the equities market, increasing the demand side of the supply/demand equation. The June NYSE Index Seasonal Chart shows the power of this move. This trade has earned profits of $38,775 since 1988.

PERFORMANCE HISTORY (1988-1997)

Total Profit $38,775
Total Years Examined 10
Profit Years 9 (90%)
Loss Years 1 (10%)
Inactive Years 0
Average Profit $4,325
Average Loss $150
Profit-to-Loss Ratio 28.8
Total Profits/Total Losses 259.5

JUNE NYSE INDEX
1988 - 1997

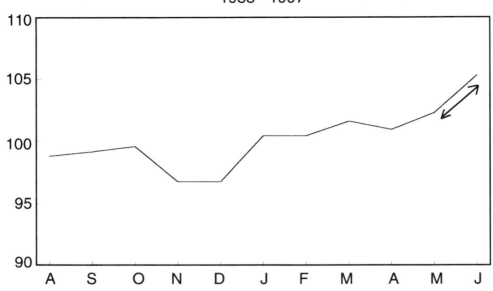

Rules for NYSE Index Trade #1:

1. Enters long June NYSE Index from the second trading day of May through the first trading day of June.

2. Place a long entry stop 1 tick (5 points) above the 5-day high. Move this entry stop as needed.

3. When filled, place a protective sell stop 5 points under the low of the last 3 trading days.

4. When the low of the last 12 trading days is equal to or greater than the entry price, move the stop to 5 points under the 12 day low. Continue raising this stop as needed.

5. Exit this trade on the close of the first trading day after June 4th.

Historical Results for NYSE Index Trade #1
June NYSE Index

YXM	ENTRY DATE	L/S	PRICE	EXIT DATE	EXIT METHOD	PRICE	TRADE P/L	YEARLY P/L
1988	05/16/88	L	146.50	05/18/88	PROTS	142.40	$ (2,050)	
	05/31/88	L	144.75	06/06/88	DATEX	151.20	$ 3,225	$ 1,175
1989	05/12/89	L	174.85	06/05/89	DATEX	180.05	$ 2,600	$ 2,600
1990	05/02/90	L	184.15	06/05/90	DATEX	200.40	$ 8,125	$ 8,125
1991	05/09/91	L	209.80	05/10/91	PROTS	206.05	$ (1,875)	
	05/21/91	L	206.20	06/05/91	DATEX	211.15	$ 2,475	$ 600
1992	05/04/92	L	228.65	06/05/92	DATEX	228.35	$ (150)	$ (150)
1993	05/04/93	L	244.60	06/07/93	DATEX	246.60	$ 1,000	$ 1,000
1994	05/17/94	L	247.85	06/06/94	DATEX	254.15	$ 3,150	$ 3,150
1995	05/03/95	L	278.70	06/05/95	DATEX	288.20	$ 4,750	$ 4,750
1996	05/10/96	L	350.10	06/05/96	DATEX	363.55	$ 6,725	$ 6,725
1997	05/02/97	L	421.55	06/05/97	DATEX	443.15	$ 10,800	$ 10,800

TOTAL $ 38,775

Exit Legend:

DATEX = Exit Date
PROTS = Protective Stop
PSTOP = Profit Stop
REV   = Reverse Entry

NYSE STOCK INDEX TRADE #2

Stock and mutual fund investors all know that late fall and winter is the time of the year when the equity indices make the greatest profits. Retirement money flowing into the equity markets fuels the uptrend. The March NYSE Seasonal Chart shows an almost perfect uptrend starting from the November/ December time period and ending as the contract expires. Mega-Seasonals NYSE Index Trade #2 has an excellent history. Nine of the last 11 years have been profitable, to the tune of $65,005.

PERFORMANCE HISTORY (1988-1998)

Total Profit... $65,005
Total Years Examined 11
Profit Years 9 (82%)
Loss Years 2 (18%)
Inactive Years 0
Average Profit.. $7,967
Average Loss $3,350
Profit-to-Loss Ratio 2.4
Total Profits/Total Losses............................ 10.7

MARCH NYSE INDEX
1988 - 1998

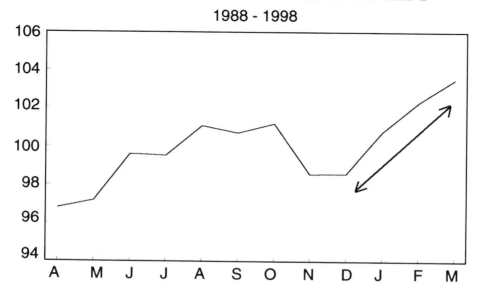

Rules for NYSE Index Trade #2:

1. Enters long March NYSE Index from the second trading day of November through the last trading day of January.

2. Place a long entry stop 5 points (1 tick) above the high of the last 12 trading days. Move this stop as needed.

3. When filled, place a protective sell stop 25 points under the low of the last 2 trading days.

4. When the low of the last 30 trading days is equal to or greater than the entry price, move the stop to 5 points under the 30 day low. Raise this stop as necessary.

5. This trade does not have a set exit date. Keep moving the trailing stop in #4 until the March NYSE goes off the board. This contract is settled in cash, so you will automatically exit this trade at the very last price.

Historical Results for NYSE Index Trade #2
March NYSE Index

YXH	ENTRY DATE	L/S	PRICE	EXIT DATE	EXIT METHOD	PRICE	TRADE P/L	YEARLY P/L
1988	12/15/87	L	137.50	03/17/88	DATEX	152.60	$ 7,550	$ 7,550
1989	11/30/88	L	155.05	03/16/89	DATEX	168.55	$ 6,750	$ 6,750
1990	11/15/89	L	192.10	01/12/90	PROTS	189.30	$ (1,400)	$ (1,400)
1991	11/12/90	L	174.40	03/15/91	DATEX	204.90	$ 15,250	$ 15,250
1992	11/08/91	L	219.60	11/15/91	PROTS	215.50	$ (2,050)	
	12/13/91	L	212.55	02/18/92	PSTOP	225.20	$ 6,325	$ 4,275
1993	11/03/92	L	232.50	11/04/92	PROTS	229.95	$ (1,275)	
	11/11/92	L	232.80	03/18/93	DATEX	249.05	$ 8,125	$ 6,850
1994	12/06/93	L	257.95	02/18/94	PSTOP	259.10	$ 575	$ 575
1995	12/15/94	L	251.35	03/17/95	DATEX	268.18	$ 8,415	$ 8,415
1996	11/08/95	L	317.80	01/10/96	PSTOP	323.05	$ 2,625	
	01/26/96	L	333.25	03/14/96	DATEX	343.40	$ 5,075	$ 7,700
1997	11/06/96	L	384.95	03/21/97	DATEX	413.63	$ 14,340	$ 14,340
1998	11/20/97	L	505.45	12/19/97	PROTS	495.55	$ (4,950)	
	12/31/97	L	516.05	12/31/97	OPEN	515.35	$ (350)	$ (5,300)

TOTAL $ 65,005

Exit Legend:

DATEX = Exit Date
PROTS = Protective Stop
PSTOP = Profit Stop
REV   = Reverse Entry

NYSE INDEX TRADE #3

The NYSE Index Trade #3 is an expanded time period version of the well-known "Santa Claus Rally." The March NYSE Seasonal Chart shows the strength of this uptrend. This trend is driven by mutual fund managers adding window dressing to their portfolios for the year-end report. Mega-Seasonals NYSE Index Trade #3 has made profits of $36,000 since 1988.

PERFORMANCE HISTORY (1988-1998)

Total Profit...$36,000
Total Years Examined 11
Profit Years 10 (91%)
Loss Years 1 (9%)
Inactive Years 0
Average Profit..............................$3,905
Average Loss $3,050
Profit-to-Loss Ratio 1.3
Total Profits/Total Losses............................12.8

MARCH NYSE INDEX
1988 - 1998

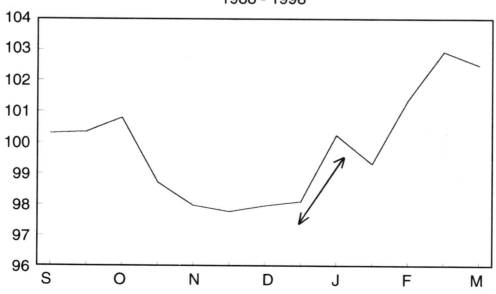

Rules for NYSE Index Trade #3:

1. Enters long March NYSE Index from December 15th through January 17th.

2. Place a long entry stop 5 points above the high of the last four trading days. Move this entry stop as necessary.

3. When filled, place a protective sell stop 5 points under the low of the last 3 trading days.

4. When the low of the last 5 days is equal to or greater than the entry price, raise your stop to 5 points under the 5-day low. Raise this stop as needed.

5. There is no date exit for this trade. Just continue raising the stop mentioned in #4.

Historical Results for NYSE Index Trade #3
March NYSE Index

YXH	ENTRY DATE	L/S	PRICE	EXIT DATE	EXIT METHOD	PRICE	TRADE P/L	YEARLY P/L
1988	12/15/87	L	137.50	02/05/88	PSTOP	140.60	$ 1,550	$ 1,550
1989	12/19/88	L	157.30	01/03/89	PROTS	155.40	$ (950)	
	01/04/89	L	158.90	02/09/89	PSTOP	166.25	$ 3,675	$ 2,725
1990	12/26/89	L	194.30	01/08/90	PSTOP	195.15	$ 425	$ 425
1991	12/18/90	L	182.70	12/20/90	PROTS	178.50	$ (2,100)	
	01/16/91	L	173.45	02/26/91	PSTOP	198.85	$ 12,700	$ 10,600
1992	12/20/91	L	213.85	01/10/92	PSTOP	228.90	$ 7,525	
	01/14/92	L	232.40	01/21/92	PROTS	228.35	$ (2,025)	$ 5,500
1993	12/18/92	L	240.50	01/07/93	PROTS	236.85	$ (1,825)	
	01/14/93	L	238.70	02/16/93	PSTOP	244.60	$ 2,950	$ 1,125
1994	12/20/93	L	258.55	12/31/93	PSTOP	258.95	$ 200	
	01/07/94	L	260.25	01/24/94	PSTOP	261.65	$ 700	$ 900
1995	12/15/94	L	250.95	01/03/95	PSTOP	251.60	$ 325	
	01/06/95	L	253.85	01/11/95	PROTS	251.10	$ (1,375)	
	01/13/95	L	254.65	03/06/95	PSTOP	262.00	$ 3,675	$ 2,625
1996	12/22/95	L	330.25	01/10/96	PROTS	325.35	$ (2,450)	
	01/16/96	L	326.20	02/16/96	PSTOP	347.30	$ 10,550	$ 8,100
1997	12/19/96	L	390.80	12/31/96	PSTOP	394.40	$ 1,800	
	01/07/97	L	400.45	01/23/97	PSTOP	407.85	$ 3,700	$ 5,500
1998	12/17/97	L	515.25	12/19/97	PROTS	502.40	$ (6,425)	
	12/30/97	L	508.60	12/31/97	OPEN	515.35	$ 3,375	$ (3,050)

TOTAL $ 36,000

Exit Legend:

DATEX = Exit Date
PROTS = Protective Stop
PSTOP = Profit Stop
REV   = Reverse Entry

- Chapter 17 -

10 YEAR TREASURY NOTES

Futures on the 10 Year Treasury Note began trading on the Chicago Board of Trade in 1982. Options began trading in 1985. The face value of the Board of Trade T-Note contract is $100,000. A half-sized, $50,000 contract, trades on the MidAmerica Commodity Exchange. The 10 Year T-Note is approximately two-thirds as volatile as the 30 Year T-Bond.

The U. S. Government is the seller (supplier) of the 10 Year Treasury Note. As in the 30 Year T-Bond, the Federal Government sells large amounts of T-Notes to meet government spending and tax refunds during the first few months of the new year. These sales decline in early May as tax payments flood the government coffers.

Investors control the demand side of the 10 Year T-Note market. Investments in these T-Notes are at their lowest during the first part of the year.

The 10 Year T-Note price responds to the many reports issued by the government. Some of these reports are New Home Sales and Existing Home Sales, GDP, Consumer and Producer Price Indexes and Employment/ Unemployment figures.

10 YEAR T-NOTE TRADE #1

Just as in the 30 Year Treasury Bond market, the 10 Year T-Note has a very strong downward trend beginning in the January through February time period. But every so often this trend turns Counter-Seasonal and rallies. This is why *Mega-Seasonals* trades both sides of the market, profiting from the move that develops. This trade mirrors the 30 Year Treasury Bond Trade #1, but can be traded with a smaller futures account. Mega-Seasonals 10 Year T-Note Trade #1 has been profitable in all but one year for a total profit of $50,594.

PERFORMANCE HISTORY (1983-1997)

Total Profit $50,594
Total Years Examined 15
Profit Years 14 (93%)
Loss Years 1 (7%)
Inactive Years 0
Average Profit $3,848
Average Loss $3,282
Profit-to-Loss Ratio 1.2
Total Profits/Total Losses 16.4

JUNE 10 YEAR T-NOTES
1983 - 1997

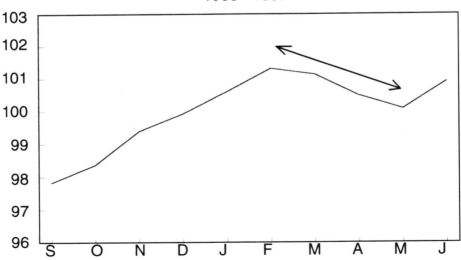

Rules for 10 Year T-Note Trade #1:

1. Enters long and short June 10 Year T-Notes from the first trading day after January 15th through February 27th.

2. Place a long entry stop 2 ticks above the 14 day high and a short entry stop 2 ticks below the 14 day low. Change these entry stops as needed.

3. When filled:
    On long: Place a protective sell stop 1 tick below the low of the last 6 trading days.
    On short: Place a protective buy stop 1 tick above the high of the last 6 trading days.

    Remember to continue entering the opposite entry as described in #2 until you are no longer in the trade entry window. Should you already have entered a trade via #2 and the reverse entry price is greater than either your protective sell stop or profit stop (for longs), use the entry price to exit the current trade so that your new position is short. Of course, should you presently be short, adjust the protective buy stop or profit stop.

4. If long: When the low of the last 21 trading days is equal to or greater than the entry price, raise your stop to 1 tick under the 21 day low.
    If short: When the high of the last 21 trading days is equal to or less than the entry price, raise your stop to 1 tick above the 21 day high.
    Continue changing the stop as necessary.

5. Exit trade on the close of the first trading day after May 8th.

Historical Results for T-Note Trade #1
June T-Note

TYM	ENTRY DATE	L/S	PRICE	EXIT DATE	EXIT METHOD	PRICE	TRADE P/L	YEARLY P/L
1983	01/21/83	S	83 18	02/16/83	REV	82 28	$ 688	
	02/16/83	L	82 28	05/09/83	DATEX	86 14	$ 3,563	$ 4,251
1984	02/06/84	S	79 07	05/09/84	DATEX	73 25	$ 5,438	$ 5,438
1985	01/18/85	L	80 09	02/08/85	REV	79 31	$ (313)	
	02/08/85	S	79 31	03/26/85	PSTOP	79 00	$ 969	$ 656
1986	01/29/86	L	92 13	04/25/86	PSTOP	100 26	$ 8,406	$ 8,406
1987	01/19/87	L	104 03	01/26/87	PROTS	103 07	$ (875)	
	02/02/87	S	103 04	02/24/87	REV	103 30	$ (813)	
	02/24/87	L	103 30	03/30/87	PROTS	102 11	$ (1,594)	$ (3,282)
1988	01/20/88	L	94 29	03/18/88	PSTOP	96 05	$ 1,250	$ 1,250
1989	01/18/89	L	93 18	02/09/89	REV	93 06	$ (375)	
	02/09/89	S	93 06	04/03/89	PSTOP	92 16	$ 688	$ 313
1990	01/18/90	S	97 25	05/09/90	DATEX	94 00	$ 3,781	$ 3,781
1991	01/25/91	L	99 11	02/22/91	REV	99 17	$ 188	
	02/22/91	S	99 17	04/04/91	PSTOP	99 00	$ 531	$ 719
1992	01/24/92	S	102 23	04/03/92	PSTOP	102 18	$ 156	$ 156
1993	01/19/93	L	106 31	05/10/93	DATEX	113 02	$ 6,094	$ 6,094
1994	01/28/94	L	113 27	02/03/94	PROTS	112 21	$ (1,188)	
	02/04/94	S	112 10	05/09/94	DATEX	102 22	$ 9,625	$ 8,437
1995	01/27/95	L	100 22	05/09/95	DATEX	108 15	$ 7,781	$ 7,781
1996	01/18/96	L	114 14	02/16/96	REV	113 09	$ (1,156)	
	02/16/96	S	113 09	05/09/96	DATEX	106 14	$ 6,844	$ 5,688
1997	01/27/97	S	107 01	01/31/97	PROTS	108 09	$ (1,250)	
	02/03/97	L	108 11	02/26/97	REV	108 12	$ 31	
	02/26/97	S	108 12	04/29/97	PSTOP	106 08	$ 2,125	$ 906

TOTAL $ 50,594

Exit Legend:

DATEX = Exit Date
PROTS = Protective Stop
PSTOP = Profit Stop
REV   = Reverse Entry

10 YEAR T-NOTE TRADE #2

As you can see from the September T-Note Seasonal Chart, there is a powerful uptrend beginning in May. The power behind this trade is the lack of the Federal Government's selling of T-Notes. With taxes flooding the Government's bank vaults there is not as much need to sell debt instruments. With less selling than normal, prices rise. Mega-Seasonals T-Note Trade #2 has been profitable 82% of the years traded for a profit of $20,531.

PERFORMANCE HISTORY (1983-1997)

Total Profit $20,531
Total Years Examined 15
Profit Years 9 (82%)
Loss Years 2 (18%)
Inactive Years 4
Average Profit $2,472
Average Loss $860
Profit-to-Loss Ratio 2.9
Total Profits/Total Losses 12.9

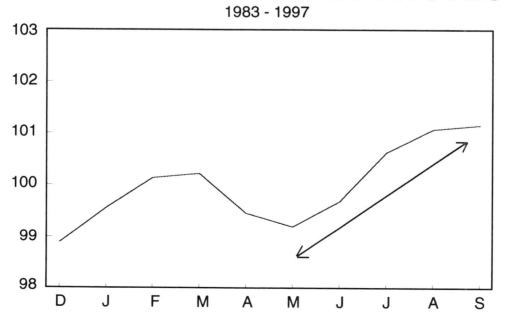

SEPTEMBER 10 YEAR T-NOTES
1983 - 1997

Rules for 10 Year T-Note Trade #2:

1. Enters long September 10 Year T-Note from the first trading day after May 1st through June 4th.

2. Place a long entry stop 6 ticks above the high of the last 12 trading days. Move this entry stop as needed.

3. When filled, place a protective sell stop 1 tick below the low of the last 4 trading days.

4. When the low of the last 12 trading days is equal to or greater than the entry price, raise the stop to 1 tick below the 12 day low. Raise this stop as the 12 day low increases.

5. Exit trade on the close of the first trading day after June 13th.

Historical Results for T-Note Trade #2
September T-Note

TYU	ENTRY DATE	L/S	PRICE	EXIT DATE	EXIT METHOD	PRICE	TRADE P/L	YEARLY P/L
1983	05/04/83	L	86 07	05/16/83	PROTS	85 14	$ (781)	$ (781)
1984	N/T						$ N/T	$ N/T
1985	05/07/85	L	81 14	06/14/85	DATEX	87 16	$ 6,063	$ 6,063
1986	N/T						$ N/T	$ N/T
1987	05/29/87	L	95 20	06/15/87	DATEX	97 04	$ 1,500	$ 1,500
1988	N/T						$ N/T	$ N/T
1989	05/05/89	L	94 04	05/09/89	PROTS	93 01	$ (1,094)	
	05/12/89	L	94 14	06/14/89	DATEX	98 14	$ 4,000	$ 2,906
1990	05/11/90	L	94 24	06/14/90	DATEX	97 09	$ 2,531	$ 2,531
1991	05/30/91	L	98 23	06/04/91	PROTS	97 25	$ (938)	$ (938)
1992	05/06/92	L	101 12	06/15/92	DATEX	103 10	$ 1,938	$ 1,938
1993	06/03/93	L	111 18	06/14/93	DATEX	112 02	$ 500	$ 500
1994	05/18/94	L	104 20	06/14/94	DATEX	105 13	$ 781	$ 781
1995	05/03/95	L	105 20	06/14/95	DATEX	110 17	$ 4,906	$ 4,906
1996	N/T						$ N/T	$ N/T
1997	05/09/97	L	107 04	06/16/97	DATEX	108 08	$ 1,125	$ 1,125

TOTAL $ 20,531

Exit Legend:

DATEX = Exit Date
PROTS = Protective Stop
PSTOP = Profit Stop
REV   = Reverse Entry

- Chapter 18 -

PORK BELLIES

Pork Bellies are uncured bacon from the underside of the hog. Each hog provides two of these, thus the plural name "bellies." Pork Bellies (40,000 lbs.) began trading on the Chicago Mercantile Exchange in 1966, with options on Pork Belly Futures commencing trading in 1986. Once the most beloved trading vehicle of speculators and day traders because of the large and fast moves, now bellies have been overshadowed by the financial markets.

Traders watching the supply factors of the pork belly market should keep an eye on the supply factors for hogs, much as soybean oil traders should be alert to any changes in the fundamentals of the soybean market. The size of the pig crop and the weight of the hogs slaughtered are both of importance. There is a consistent seasonal pattern to hog production. The spring pig crop yields the largest percent of pork belly production. This crop is marketed in the fall. Thus pork belly production peaks in the late fall and early winter and bottoms out in the June through August time period.

On the demand side, bacon consumption is relatively stable with the exception of extremes in price. When prices are at very high levels, demand declines until prices fall back to more reasonable prices.

The reports a pork belly trader should watch are the same reports watched when trading hogs; Cold Storage being of greatest importance. Like hogs, pork bellies can and will react violently to any surprises in these reports. It is not rare for a surprise report to reverse the direction of the market. At times this reversal is in "limit bid" days. Always watch carefully when trading bellies and be well margined.

PORK BELLY TRADE #1

The August Pork Belly Seasonal Chart has a long-term downtrend from October through July. This represents the active hog slaughter and the buildup of pork bellies that normally occur during this time frame. This downtrend can become dramatic around April as prices drop "like a rock." Mega-Seasonals Pork Belly Trade #1 profits greatly from this decline. In the last 21 years this trade has produced $64,640 in profits (based on a 40,000 lb. contract).

PERFORMANCE HISTORY (1977-1997)

Total Profit..$64,640
Total Years Examined 21
Profit Years 18 (86%)
Loss Years 3 (14%)
Inactive Years 0
Average Profit...$3,949
Average Loss $2,147
Profit-to-Loss Ratio 1.8
Total Profits/Total Losses............................11.0

AUGUST PORK BELLIES

1977 - 1997

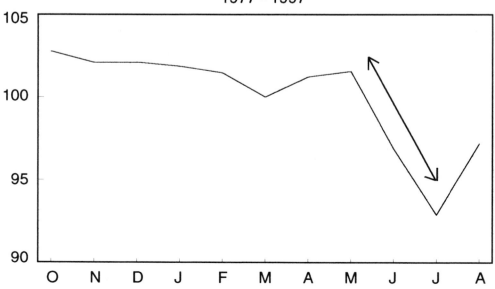

Rules for Pork Belly Trade #1:

1. Enters short August Pork Bellies from the first trading day of April through the last trading day of June.

2. Place a short entry stop 2 ticks (5 points) below the low of the last 14 trading days. Move this entry stop as necessary.

3. When filled, place a protective buy stop 1 tick above the high of the last 4 trading days.

4. When the high of the last 13 trading days is equal to or lower than the entry price, lower your stop to 1 tick above the 13 day high. Lower this stop as needed.

5. Exit trade on the close of the first trading day after July 29th.

Historical Results for Pork Belly Trade #1
August Pork Bellies

PBQ	ENTRY DATE	L/S	PRICE	EXIT DATE	EXIT METHOD	PRICE	TRADE P/L	YEARLY P/L
1977	05/18/77	S	57.700	06/29/77	PSTOP	54.975	$ 1,090	$ 1,090
1978	04/12/78	S	74.900	05/15/78	PSTOP	72.500	$ 960	
	05/19/78	S	66.000	07/17/78	PSTOP	50.275	$ 6,290	$ 7,250
1979	04/03/79	S	52.300	04/10/79	PROTS	55.425	$ (1,250)	
	05/07/79	S	52.750	07/30/79	DATEX	27.900	$ 9,940	$ 8,690
1980	04/01/80	S	35.475	06/23/80	PSTOP	32.750	$ 1,090	$ 1,090
1981	04/29/81	S	55.000	05/22/81	PSTOP	52.000	$ 1,200	
	06/23/81	S	51.025	07/28/81	DATEX	45.475	$ 2,220	$ 3,420
1982	05/24/82	S	81.100	07/01/82	PSTOP	74.025	$ 2,830	$ 2,830
1983	04/18/83	S	65.050	06/26/83	PSTOP	60.375	$ 1,870	$ 1,870
1984	04/17/84	S	67.500	06/11/84	PSTOP	67.000	$ 200	
	06/27/84	S	63.350	07/30/84	DATEX	51.900	$ 4,580	$ 4,780
1985	04/02/85	S	68.450	05/22/85	PSTOP	65.950	$ 1,000	
	06/24/85	S	63.800	07/30/85	DATEX	50.700	$ 5,240	$ 6,240
1986	04/01/86	S	55.650	04/28/86	PSTOP	53.775	$ 750	$ 750
1987	05/13/87	S	65.550	05/28/87	PROTS	69.275	$ (1,490)	
	06/26/87	S	72.825	07/08/87	PROTS	76.500	$ (1,470)	$ (2,960)
1988	04/05/88	S	53.050	05/11/88	PSTOP	52.425	$ 250	
	06/09/88	S	50.900	07/22/88	PSTOP	38.800	$ 4,840	$ 5,090
1989	04/03/89	S	36.000	05/09/89	PSTOP	32.575	$ 1,370	
	05/26/89	S	31.100	07/31/89	DATEX	25.075	$ 2,410	$ 3,780
1990	05/14/90	S	61.150	07/30/90	DATEX	49.225	$ 4,770	$ 4,770
1991	04/08/91	S	59.950	07/30/91	DATEX	43.150	$ 6,720	$ 6,720
1992	04/13/92	S	33.000	05/07/92	PROTS	34.425	$ (570)	
	05/26/92	S	32.100	07/17/92	PSTOP	29.825	$ 910	$ 340
1993	04/06/93	S	46.000	04/14/93	PROTS	50.675	$ (1,870)	
	04/19/93	S	45.450	07/02/93	PSTOP	35.400	$ 4,020	$ 2,150
1994	04/06/94	S	52.500	06/16/94	PSTOP	42.275	$ 4,090	
	06/27/94	S	38.700	08/01/94	DATEX	27.175	$ 4,610	$ 8,700
1995	04/03/95	S	37.500	05/23/95	PSTOP	37.975	$ (190)	
	06/05/95	S	33.900	06/08/95	PROTS	36.775	$ (1,150)	$ (1,340)
1996	05/20/96	S	80.100	07/03/96	PROTS	76.300	$ 1,520	$ 1,520
1997	05/14/97	S	85.550	05/16/97	PROTS	91.225	$ (2,270)	
	05/30/97	S	85.400	06/30/97	PSTOP	85.075	$ 130	$ (2,140)

TOTAL $ 64,640

Exit Legend:

DATEX = Exit Date
PROTS = Protective Stop
PSTOP = Profit Stop
REV   = Reverse Entry

PORK BELLY TRADE #2

Pork Belly Trade #2 is the reverse of Pork Belly Trade #1. It might even be called "a dead cat bounce." After many months of large hog marketings and large quantities of Pork Bellies going into storage, the supply of hogs coming to market dries up. This is just in time for the seasonal growth in demand for summer food favorites like bacon, lettuce and tomato sandwiches. You can see this in the February Pork Belly Seasonal Chart. Mega-Seasonals Pork Belly Trade #2 has produced $20,030 in profits over the last 21 years.

PERFORMANCE HISTORY (1978-1998)

Total Profit	$20,030	
Total Years Examined	21	
Profit Years	11	(65%)
Loss Years	6	(35%)
Inactive Years	4	
Average Profit	$2,652	
Average Loss	$1,523	
Profit-to-Loss Ratio	1.7	
Total Profits/Total Losses	3.2	

FEBRUARY PORK BELLIES

1978 - 1998

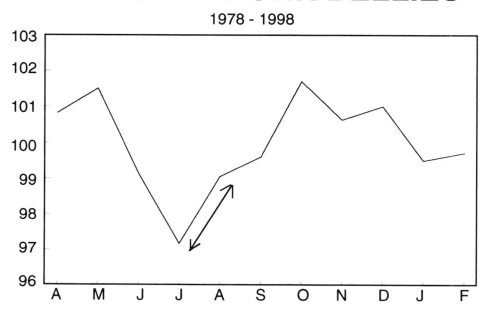

Rules for Pork Belly Trade #2:

1. Enters long February Pork Bellies from June 15th through the last trading day of July.

2. Place a long entry stop 1 tick (2 1/2 points) above the high of the last 18 trading days. As this high drops, lower your entry price.

3. When filled, place a protective sell stop 12 1/2 points below the low of the last 5 trading days.

4. When the low of the last 8 trading days is equal to or greater than the entry price, raise your stop to 1 tick under the 8-day low. Raise this stop as needed.

5. Exit this trade on the close of the first trading day after October 16th.

Historical Results for Pork Belly Trade #2
February Pork Bellies

PBG	ENTRY DATE	L/S	PRICE	EXIT DATE	EXIT METHOD	PRICE	TRADE P/L	YEARLY P/L
1978	07/06/77	L	53.725	07/08/77	PROTS	50.875	$ (1,140)	$ (1,140)
1979	07/27/78	L	58.800	10/17/78	DATEX	71.600	$ 5,120	$ 5,120
1980	N/T						$ N/T	$ N/T
1981	06/17/80	L	48.275	07/23/80	PSTOP	55.925	$ 3,060	$ 3,060
1982	N/T						$ N/T	$ N/T
1983	07/22/82	L	76.700	09/14/82	PSTOP	84.175	$ 2,990	$ 2,990
1984	07/21/83	L	58.750	08/29/83	PSTOP	63.625	$ 1,950	$ 1,950
1985	06/15/84	L	79.825	06/25/84	PROTS	77.750	$ (830)	$ (830)
1986	06/18/85	L	75.000	06/20/85	PROTS	73.000	$ (800)	$ (800)
1987	06/19/86	L	61.925	08/06/86	PSTOP	74.400	$ 4,990	$ 4,990
1988	07/06/87	L	62.825	08/12/87	PSTOP	63.225	$ 160	$ 160
1989	N/T						$ N/T	$ N/T
1990	06/20/89	L	51.100	07/06/89	PROTS	45.750	$ (2,140)	$ (2,140)
1991	07/31/90	L	57.025	10/17/90	DATEX	66.700	$ 3,870	$ 3,870
1992	07/29/91	L	49.225	08/13/91	PROTS	46.475	$ (1,100)	$ (1,100)
1993	07/30/92	L	40.425	10/19/92	DATEX	44.800	$ 1,750	$ 1,750
1994	07/01/93	L	41.675	08/09/93	PSTOP	49.875	$ 3,280	$ 3,280
1995	N/T						$ N/T	$ N/T
1996	06/20/95	L	52.000	07/05/95	PSTOP	52.150	$ 60	
	07/28/95	L	54.775	10/06/95	PSTOP	58.925	$ 1,660	$ 1,720
1997	07/08/96	L	81.925	09/17/96	PROTS	74.100	$ (3,130)	$ (3,130)
1998	07/29/97	L	73.025	08/12/97	PSTOP	73.725	$ 280	$ 280

TOTAL $ 20,030

Exit Legend:

DATEX = Exit Date
PROTS = Protective Stop
PSTOP = Profit Stop
REV   = Reverse Entry

- Chapter 19 -

STANDARD & POOR'S 500 STOCK INDEX

Futures trading on the Standard and Poor's (S&P) Stock Index began trading on the Chicago Mercantile Exchange's Index and Option Market Division in 1982. In 1983, options on the futures were added. The S&P 500 Index is the standard benchmark for the entire United States equity market. The index is a collection of the value of the 500 largest U. S. Corporation's stocks. It has been compiled by the Standard and Poor's Corporation since 1957. The total value of the S&P 500 Index was $500 times the index until late 1997 when the value of the index was halved to $250 times the index. Also a new E-mini S&P contract began computerized trading with a value of $50 times the index. This allows much smaller accounts to participate in the S&P Index market.

The supply side of this index is relatively static, with demand being the major influence. Generally, low unemployment, low inflation, increasing housing starts, high and rising consumer confidence and a good economy with low interest rates propels this market upward. Enormously important in this price discovery equation are interest rates and the direction of interest rate trends. It is quite normal for both interest rate futures and equity index futures to trend in the same direction, although at times these futures do "disconnect." Should the economic situation change dramatically, the S&P Index futures will "tank" and prices will drop.

The U. S. Government issues many reports that affect the S&P Index. Some of these reports are Unemployment, Wholesale Trade, Manufacturing and Trade Inventories, Producer and Consumer Price Indexes, Retail Sales, Industrial Production, Trade Balance, Export Sales, Housing Starts and Durable Goods Orders, to name just a few.

S&P 500 INDEX TRADE #1

The June S&P Seasonal Chart shows a strong trend from mid-November through June, with a temporary consolidation range from March through May. Mega-Seasonal S&P 500 Trade #1 profits from the upside breakout of the price consolidation range from early May through June. The normal drop in interest rates during this time period has much to do with this movement. Investment money abandons the interest rate markets and helps to fuel the rally in equities. Add to this the funds flowing into IRA's and 401K Retirement Plans and you generate a super rally. The S&P 500 Index Trade #1 has earned $75,575 since 1983 based on the value of the index at the $500 multiplier.

PERFORMANCE HISTORY (1983-1997)

Total Profit $75,575
Total Years Examined 15
Profit Years 13 (87%)
Loss Years 2 (13%)
Inactive Years 0
Average Profit $6,048
Average Loss $1,525
Profit-to-Loss Ratio 4.0
Total Profits/Total Losses 25.8

JUNE S&P 500
1983 - 1997

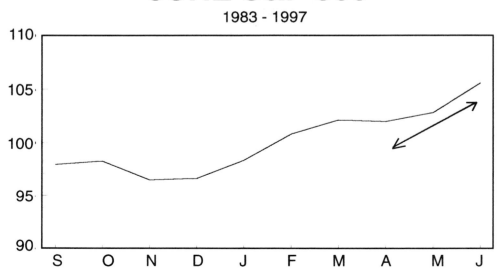

Rules for S&P Index Trade #1:

1. Enters long June S&P Index from the second trading day of May through the first trading day of June.

2. Place a long entry stop 1 tick (10 points) above the high of the last 5 trading days. Move this stop as needed.

3. When filled, place a protective sell stop 1 tick (10 points) below the low of the last 5 trading days.

4. When the low of the last 12 trading days is equal to or greater than the entry price, raise your stop to 1 tick under the 12 day low. Raise this stop as the 12 day low increases.

5. Exit this trade on the close of the first trading day after June 3rd.

Historical Results for S & P 500 Index Trade #1
June S & P

SPM	ENTRY DATE	L/S	PRICE	EXIT DATE	EXIT METHOD	PRICE	TRADE P/L	YEARLY P/L
1983	05/04/83	L	164.75	06/06/83	DATEX	165.45	$ 350	$ 350
1984	05/02/84	L	162.95	05/11/84	PROTS	158.80	$ (2,075)	$ (2,075)
1985	05/07/85	L	181.40	06/04/85	DATEX	190.30	$ 4,450	$ 4,450
1986	05/09/86	L	238.50	05/15/86	PROTS	233.20	$ (2,650)	
	05/22/86	L	237.65	06/04/86	DATEX	244.40	$ 3,375	$ 725
1987	05/04/87	L	291.20	06/04/87	DATEX	295.20	$ 2,000	$ 2,000
1988	05/16/88	L	259.15	05/18/88	PROTS	251.75	$ (3,700)	
	05/31/88	L	256.05	06/06/88	DATEX	267.85	$ 5,900	$ 2,200
1989	05/12/89	L	313.65	06/05/89	DATEX	323.00	$ 4,675	$ 4,675
1990	05/02/90	L	335.85	06/04/90	DATEX	368.75	$ 16,450	$ 16,450
1991	05/09/91	L	383.35	05/10/91	PROTS	376.75	$ (3,300)	
	05/21/91	L	376.45	06/04/91	DATEX	388.60	$ 6,075	$ 2,775
1992	05/04/92	L	415.45	06/04/92	DATEX	413.50	$ (975)	$ (975)
1993	05/04/93	L	442.65	06/04/93	DATEX	450.60	$ 3,975	$ 3,975
1994	05/17/94	L	447.55	06/06/94	DATEX	459.35	$ 5,900	$ 5,900
1995	05/03/95	L	517.30	06/05/95	DATEX	536.65	$ 9,675	$ 9,675
1996	05/10/96	L	654.35	06/04/96	DATEX	673.20	$ 9,425	$ 9,425
1997	05/02/97	L	810.05	06/04/97	DATEX	842.10	$ 16,025	$ 16,025

TOTAL $ 75,575

Exit Legend:

DATEX = Exit Date
PROTS = Protective Stop
PSTOP = Profit Stop
REV   = Reverse Entry

S&P 500 INDEX TRADE #2

If there is any doubt about the validity of financial seasonals, just look at the March S&P 500 Seasonal Chart. Talk about an obvious trend. After bottoming out in November, prices rally through March. It's been said that greater than 90% of all the total points in the S&P have been gained during this period. I can't say enough about this trade. The Mega-Seasonal S&P 500 Trade #2 has a 4.0 to 1 profit-to-loss ratio and has earned profits of $160,325 since 1984. (Based on the actual contract value at the time of the trade.)

PERFORMANCE HISTORY (1984-1998)

Total Profit... $160,325
Total Years Examined 15
Profit Years 12 (80%)
Loss Years 3 (20%)
Inactive Years 0
Average Profit..................................... $14,250
Average Loss $3,558
Profit-to-Loss Ratio 4.0
Total Profits/Total Losses............................ 16.0

MARCH S&P 500

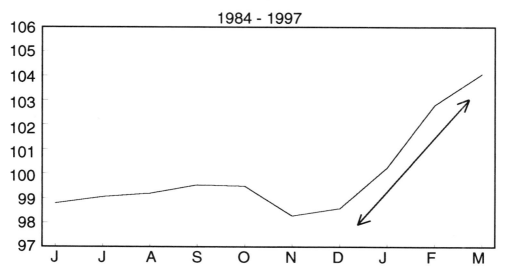

1984 - 1997

Rules for S&P Index Trade #2

1. Enters long March S&P Index from November 1st through January 31.

2. Place a long entry stop 10 points (1 tick) above the high of the last 16 trading days. Move this entry stop as necessary.

3. When filled, place a protective stop 10 points below the low of the last 5 trading days.

4. When the low of the last 30 trading days is equal to or greater than the entry price, raise your stop to 1 tick under the 30 day low. Raise this stop as needed.

5. Exit trade on the close of the first trading day after March 17th. Should the March S&P contract go off the board before March 17th it will be settled for cash at the last price.

Historical Results for S & P Index Trade #2
March S & P Index ($500 times index unless otherwise noted)

SPH	ENTRY DATE	L/S	PRICE	EXIT DATE	EXIT METHOD	PRICE	TRADE P/L	YEARLY P/L
1984	11/29/83	L	170.95	12/02/83	PROTS	167.70	$ (1,625)	
	01/04/84	L	168.45	01/27/84	PROTS	165.55	$ (1,450)	$ (3,075)
1985	12/18/84	L	171.70	03/14/85	PSTOP	177.85	$ 3,075	$ 3,075
1986	11/01/85	L	192.15	01/21/86	PSTOP	204.85	$ 6,350	
	01/31/86	L	213.75	03/18/86	DATEX	236.45	$ 11,350	$ 17,700
1987	11/03/86	L	246.00	11/18/86	PROTS	238.90	$ (3,550)	
	11/24/86	L	249.05	03/18/87	DATEX	292.65	$ 21,800	$ 18,250
1988	12/18/87	L	250.10	03/18/88	DATEX	270.80	$ 9,350	$ 9,350
1989	12/05/88	L	278.15	03/16/89	DATEX	299.70	$ 10,775	$ 10,775
1990	11/24/89	L	348.35	01/12/90	PSTOP	342.50	$ (2,925)	$ (2,925)
1991	11/12/90	L	321.35	03/15/91	DATEX	374.90	$ 26,775	$ 26,775
1992	11/08/91	L	398.55	11/15/91	PROTS	390.15	$ (4,200)	
	12/13/91	L	385.00	02/18/92	PSTOP	407.45	$ 11,225	$ 7,025
1993	11/02/92	L	421.55	03/16/93	DATEX	450.70	$ 14,575	$ 14,575
1994	12/06/93	L	468.55	02/18/94	PSTOP	459.20	$ (4,675)	$ (4,675)
1995	12/16/94	L	461.05	03/16/95	DATEX	495.75	$ 17,350	$ 17,350
1996	11/08/95	L	598.95	01/10/96	PSTOP	605.10	$ 3,075	
	01/29/96	L	624.80	03/14/96	DATEX	641.60	$ 8,400	$ 11,475
1997	11/06/96	L	725.25	03/18/97	DATEX	787.55	$ 31,150	$ 31,150
1998	11/20/97	L	965.10	12/31/97	OPEN	979.10	$ 3,500	$ 3,500*

TOTAL $ 160,325

* $250 times index

Exit Legend:

DATEX = Exit Date
PROTS = Protective Stop
PSTOP = Profit Stop
REV   = Reverse Entry

S&P 500 INDEX TRADE #3

S&P 500 Index Trade #3 could be named "the Santa Claus Rally and how to trade it!" The March S&P 500 Seasonal Chart reveals this rally quite well. Why does this rally take place? The best explanation is year-end book squaring by equity mutual fund managers and individual investors. *Mega-Seasonals* has widened the Santa Claus Rally time window of opportunity to increase entries and profits. Since 1984 this trade has been correct 87% of the time for a net profit of $87,500. (Based on the actual contract value at the time of the trade.)

PERFORMANCE HISTORY (1984-1998)

Total Profit $87,500
Total Years Examined 15
Profit Years 13 (87%)
Loss Years 2 (13%)
Inactive Years 0
Average Profit $7,379
Average Loss $4,213
Profit-to-Loss Ratio 1.8
Total Profits/Total Losses 11.4

MARCH S&P 500
1984 - 1998

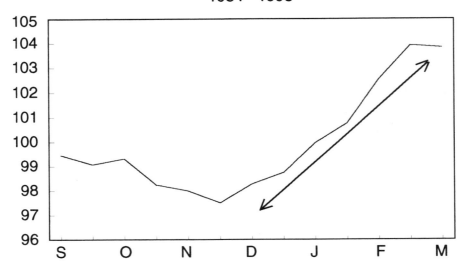

Rules for S&P Index Trade #3:

1. Enters long March S&P Index from December 15th through January 17th.

2. Place a long entry stop 1 tick (10 points) above the high of the last 4 trading days. As the 4-day high decreases, lower your entry stop.

3. When filled, place a protective sell stop 1 tick (10 points) below the low of the last 5 trading days.

4. When the low of the last 5 trading days is equal to or greater than the entry price, raise your stop to 1 tick below the 5-day low. Raise this as needed.

5. There is no date exit for this trade. Continue entering the profit stop until stopped out. Should you not get stopped out and the March S&P goes off the board, don't worry. This contract is settled in cash. Your trade will be closed at the last price.

Historical Results for S & P 500 Trade #3
March S & P 500 ($500 times index unless otherwise noted)

SPH	ENTRY DATE	L/S	PRICE	EXIT DATE	EXIT METHOD	PRICE	TRADE P/L	YEARLY P/L
1984	12/21/83	L	166.45	01/13/84	PSTOP	169.40	$ 1,475	$ 1,475
1985	12/18/84	L	169.70	02/21/85	PSTOP	180.75	$ 5,525	$ 5,525
1986	12/31/85	L	213.60	01/08/86	PROTS	208.55	$ (2,525)	
	01/15/86	L	208.15	01/21/86	PROTS	204.85	$ (1,650)	$ (4,175)
1987	01/05/87	L	248.60	02/10/87	PSTOP	275.45	$ 13,425	$ 13,425
1988	12/15/87	L	245.30	01/08/88	PSTOP	245.75	$ 225	
	01/15/88	L	257.00	03/10/88	PSTOP	264.50	$ 3,750	$ 3,975
1989	12/19/88	L	279.85	01/03/89	PROTS	276.75	$ (1,550)	
	01/04/89	L	282.70	02/10/89	PSTOP	296.35	$ 6,825	$ 5,275
1990	12/26/89	L	351.85	01/08/90	PSTOP	354.15	$ 1,150	$ 1,150
1991	12/21/90	L	334.55	01/02/91	PROTS	327.20	$ (3,675)	
	01/16/91	L	316.65	02/26/91	PSTOP	364.45	$ 23,900	$ 20,225
1992	12/20/91	L	388.10	01/10/92	PSTOP	416.45	$ 14,175	
	01/15/92	L	422.55	01/21/92	PROTS	414.70	$ (3,925)	$ 10,250
1993	12/17/92	L	436.60	12/30/92	PSTOP	437.55	$ 475	
	01/14/93	L	434.20	02/16/93	PSTOP	443.70	$ 4,750	$ 5,225
1994	12/20/93	L	467.50	12/31/93	PSTOP	468.45	$ 475	
	01/07/94	L	469.45	01/24/94	PSTOP	472.30	$ 1,425	$ 1,900
1995	12/15/94	L	460.05	12/30/94	PSTOP	461.85	$ 900	
	01/06/95	L	465.50	01/23/95	PSTOP	465.95	$ 225	$ 1,125
1996	12/27/95	L	620.45	01/09/96	PROTS	610.60	$ (4,925)	
	01/17/96	L	611.15	02/16/96	PSTOP	651.05	$ 19,950	$ 15,025
1997	12/19/96	L	740.65	12/31/96	PSTOP	749.25	$ 4,300	
	01/07/97	L	759.85	01/24/97	PSTOP	773.95	$ 7,050	$ 11,350
1998	12/17/97	L	985.60	12/19/97	PROTS	956.00	$ (7,400)*	
	12/30/97	L	966.50	12/31/97	OPEN	979.10	$ 3,150 *	$ (4,250)*

TOTAL $ 87,500

* $250 times index

Exit Legend:

DATEX = Exit Date
PROTS = Protective Stop
PSTOP = Profit Stop
REV   = Reverse Entry

- Chapter 20 -

SOYBEANS

Futures trading of Soybeans (5000 bu.) began on the Chicago Board of Trade in 1936. A smaller sized (1000 bu.) contract trades on the MidAmerica Commodity Exchange. Options are also traded. It is only since World War II that soybeans have become a major U. S. crop. Presently, the U. S. is the single largest exporter of soybeans and soybean products, but Brazil is rapidly growing in importance.

The supply side of the pricing equation should consider the U. S. carryover, world carryover, planting intentions and weather conditions in both the U. S. and Brazil. The weather in the Corn Belt during the months of April through May is of great importance. Should the weather conditions in the Corn Belt be too wet, not allowing the farmers access to their fields, they may switch from corn to beans, which can be planted later.

The demand side of the price realization must take into account the increasing demand for edible fats and the improved livestock feeding methods used to increase protein content. Very important to the price discovery of soybeans is the price of the two products, soybean oil and soybean meal.

The major reports to watch when trading soybeans are the Spring Planting Intentions Report, The Crop Production Reports issued throughout the growing season, Export Inspections, NOPA Crush Statistics and Grain Stocks Report.

SOYBEAN TRADE #1

The Mega-Seasonal Soybean Trade #1 is a classic pre-harvest short trade. During the early spring months, Soybeans normally rally. As the crop is planted and the growing season progresses, farmers, traders and commercials estimate the probable "new" crop of beans. Farmers begin their hedging operations around June/July sending the November "new crop" Soybean contract lower. This is supported by the November Soybean Seasonal Chart. This trade has been successful in 18 of the last 21 years, yielding $39,368 in profits.

PERFORMANCE HISTORY (1977-1997)

Total Profit..$39,368
Total Years Examined 21
Profit Years 18 (86%)
Loss Years 3 (14%)
Inactive Years 0
Average Profit...$2,474
Average Loss $1,721
Profit-to-Loss Ratio 1.4
Total Profits/Total Losses............................. 8.6

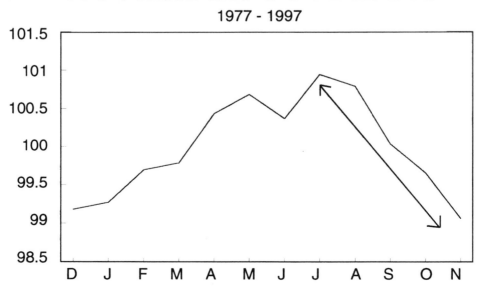

NOVEMBER SOYBEANS
1977 - 1997

Rules for Soybean Trade #1:

1. Enters short November Soybeans from the first trading day of May through the last trading day of July.

2. Place a short entry stop 3 cents below the low of the last 16 trading days. Moving this entry as necessary.

3. When filled, place a protective buy stop 1 tick above the high of the last 5 trading days.

4. When the high of the last 11 trading days is equal to or less than the entry price, lower your stop to 1 tick above the 11 day high. Lower this stop as needed.

5. Exit trade on the close of the first trading day after August 12th.

Historical Results for Soybean Trade #1
November Soybeans

SX	ENTRY DATE	L/S	PRICE	EXIT DATE	EXIT METHOD	PRICE	TRADE P/L	YEARLY P/L
1977	06/13/77	S	711.00	08/15/77	DATEX	506.75	$ 10,213	$ 10,213
1978	06/13/78	S	623.00	08/14/78	DATEX	613.75	$ 463	$ 463
1979	07/02/79	S	736.00	08/13/79	DATEX	691.75	$ 2,213	$ 2,213
1980	06/03/80	S	640.00	06/16/80	PROTS	665.75	$ (1,288)	$ (1,288)
1981	05/04/81	S	813.50	07/06/81	PSTOP	759.25	$ 2,713	$ 2,713
1982	05/27/82	S	659.25	08/13/82	DATEX	566.25	$ 4,650	$ 4,650
1983	05/09/83	S	657.00	07/01/83	PSTOP	632.75	$ 1,213	$ 1,213
1984	06/07/84	S	715.50	06/19/84	PROTS	755.25	$ (1,988)	
	07/03/84	S	697.00	08/07/84	PSTOP	640.25	$ 2,838	$ 850
1985	05/02/85	S	599.00	06/07/85	PSTOP	578.00	$ 1,050	
	06/28/85	S	556.00	07/05/85	PROTS	572.50	$ (825)	
	07/24/85	S	537.00	08/13/85	DATEX	516.00	$ 1,050	$ 1,050
1986	06/02/86	S	503.50	07/15/86	PSTOP	495.25	$ 413	$ 413
1987	06/29/87	S	548.00	07/28/87	PSTOP	535.25	$ 638	$ 638
1988	07/08/88	S	915.00	08/04/88	PSTOP	872.25	$ 2,138	$ 2,138
1989	05/16/89	S	699.00	06/14/89	PSTOP	642.25	$ 2,838	
	07/18/89	S	621.00	08/14/89	DATEX	571.00	$ 2,500	$ 5,338
1990	05/21/90	S	631.00	06/25/90	PSTOP	629.75	$ 63	
	07/20/90	S	612.50	08/09/90	PSTOP	611.75	$ 38	$ 101
1991	05/07/91	S	600.00	07/16/91	PSTOP	548.75	$ 2,563	$ 2,563
1992	07/01/92	S	602.00	08/13/92	DATEX	547.00	$ 2,750	$ 2,750
1993	06/01/93	S	594.75	06/17/93	PSTOP	593.75	$ 50	
	07/28/93	S	684.00	08/13/93	DATEX	654.00	$ 1,500	$ 1,550
1994	07/01/94	S	622.00	08/11/94	PSTOP	569.25	$ 2,638	$ 2,638
1995	05/05/95	S	588.00	05/18/95	PROTS	607.75	$ (988)	
	07/31/95	S	610.00	08/14/95	DATEX	602.75	$ 363	$ (625)
1996	05/29/96	S	757.00	07/12/96	PROTS	788.75	$ (1,588)	
	07/26/96	S	722.00	08/08/96	PROTS	755.25	$ (1,663)	$ (3,251)
1997	05/21/97	S	686.50	07/29/97	PSTOP	630.25	$ 2,813	$ 2,813

TOTAL $ 39,368

Exit Legend:

DATEX = Exit Date
PROTS = Protective Stop
PSTOP = Profit Stop
REV   = Reverse Entry

- Chapter 21 -

SOYBEAN OIL

The Chicago Board of Trade added Soybean Oil Futures (60,000 lbs.) to its trading menu in 1950. The MidAmerica Commodity Exchange trades a half-sized contract (30,000 lbs.). Options on Soybean Oil Futures began trading in 1987.

On the supply side of the price discovery equation, the trader should consider U. S. and World soybean carryover, soybean planting intentions and weather conditions during the planting and growing season in both the U. S. and South America, especially Brazil. In the U. S., rain in July and August is critical to the growth of soybeans. An early frost is disastrous for soybean oil.

The demand side of the supply/demand equation has shown little elasticity in relation to price. This is likely due to the relatively low cost of soybean oil in salad oil, shortening and margarine, the primary products that use soybean oil. After the fall harvest, demand is the most important factor in determining soybean oil prices.

Since soybean oil is one of the products of soybeans, reports concerning soybeans should be watched carefully. The Planting Intentions Report in the spring, the Crop Production Reports issued during the growing season, Export Inspection Reports, Grain and Stocks Reports and NOPA Crush Statistics are exceedingly important.

SOYBEAN OIL TRADE #1

The Soybean Oil Trade #1 is a lower risk version of the Mega-Seasonals Soybean Trade #1. This is a pre-harvest short trade. As the growing year advances and the size of the Soybean crop becomes more predictable, traders look to the Soybean Oil market to cash in on the short side. The crushers join the herd and sell their future oil supply. Thus the market declines. This can be seen on the September Soybean Oil Seasonal Chart with the downward trend often continuing into September. This Mega-Seasonal Trade has entered the market in all but 1 of the last 21 years and earned $21,036 in profits.

PERFORMANCE HISTORY (1977-1997)

Total Profit	$21,036
Total Years Examined	21
Profit Years	16 (80%)
Loss Years	4 (20%)
Inactive Years	1
Average Profit	$1,462
Average Loss	$588
Profit-to-Loss Ratio	2.5
Total Profits/Total Losses	9.9

SEPTEMBER SOYBEAN OIL
1977 - 1997

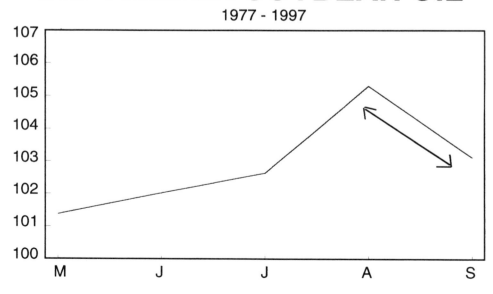

Rules for Soybean Oil Trade #1:

1. Enters short September Soybean Oil from May 15th through the last trading day of July.

2. Place a short entry stop 1 tick under the low of the last 14 trading days. Raise this entry stop as necessary.

3. When filled place a protective buy stop 1 tick above the high of the last 5 trading days.

4. When the high of the last 11 trading days is equal to or less than the entry price, lower your stop to 1 tick above the 11 day high. Lower this stop as needed.

5. Exit trade on the close of the first trading day after August 16th.

Historical Results for Soybean Oil Trade #1
September Soybean Oil

BOU	ENTRY DATE	L/S	PRICE	EXIT DATE	EXIT METHOD	PRICE	TRADE P/L	YEARLY P/L
1977	06/09/77	S	28.89	06/28/77	PSTOP	28.31	$ 348	
	07/06/77	S	24.39	08/17/77	DATEX	18.98	$ 3,246	$ 3,594
1978	06/12/78	S	24.74	08/11/78	PSTOP	23.61	$ 678	$ 678
1979	07/25/79	S	27.21	08/14/79	PSTOP	27.16	$ 30	$ 30
1980	N/T						$ N/T	$ N/T
1981	05/26/81	S	24.14	07/08/81	PSTOP	23.71	$ 258	
	07/29/81	S	23.69	08/17/81	DATEX	21.54	$ 1,290	$ 1,548
1982	05/27/82	S	20.54	08/17/82	DATEX	16.96	$ 2,148	$ 2,148
1983	05/16/83	S	19.64	07/06/83	PROTS	20.01	$ (222)	$ (222)
1984	06/01/84	S	33.49	08/07/84	PSTOP	27.26	$ 3,738	$ 3,738
1985	05/15/85	S	28.04	05/21/85	PROTS	28.85	$ (486)	
	06/04/85	S	27.49	06/06/85	PROTS	28.21	$ (432)	
	07/01/85	S	27.44	08/19/85	DATEX	22.23	$ 3,126	$ 2,208
1986	05/19/86	S	17.69	05/23/86	PROTS	18.56	$ (522)	
	06/02/86	S	17.59	07/16/86	PSTOP	16.91	$ 408	
	07/25/86	S	16.16	08/18/86	DATEX	14.28	$ 1,128	$ 1,014
1987	05/26/87	S	16.80	06/15/87	PROTS	17.51	$ (426)	
	06/22/87	S	16.75	08/03/87	PSTOP	16.50	$ 150	$ (276)
1988	07/12/88	S	29.69	08/17/88	DATEX	27.47	$ 1,332	$ 1,332
1989	05/15/89	S	23.69	07/05/89	PSTOP	22.40	$ 774	
	07/11/89	S	20.54	08/17/89	DATEX	17.91	$ 1,578	$ 2,352
1990	05/23/90	S	22.95	06/07/90	PROTS	24.11	$ (696)	
	07/11/90	S	23.61	08/17/90	DATEX	23.99	$ (228)	$ (924)
1991	05/20/91	S	20.19	05/22/91	PROTS	20.64	$ (270)	
	06/12/91	S	20.09	07/17/91	PSTOP	19.26	$ 498	$ 228
1992	06/16/92	S	20.94	08/17/92	DATEX	18.56	$ 1,428	$ 1,428
1993	06/01/93	S	21.37	06/17/93	PSTOP	21.29	$ 48	
	07/26/93	S	23.94	08/17/93	DATEX	23.18	$ 456	$ 504
1994	06/06/94	S	27.14	08/05/94	PSTOP	24.46	$ 1,608	$ 1,608
1995	05/15/95	S	24.58	05/18/95	PROTS	25.13	$ (330)	
	06/12/95	S	25.30	06/19/95	PROTS	26.76	$ (876)	
	07/27/95	S	26.89	08/17/95	DATEX	26.43	$ 276	$ (930)
1996	05/20/96	S	27.20	07/11/96	PSTOP	26.01	$ 714	
	07/22/96	S	24.77	08/19/96	DATEX	24.94	$ (102)	$ 612
1997	05/19/97	S	24.09	07/15/97	PSTOP	22.91	$ 708	
	07/21/97	S	21.69	08/18/97	DATEX	22.26	$ (342)	$ 366

TOTAL $ 21,036

Exit Legend:

DATEX = Exit Date
PROTS = Protective Stop
PSTOP = Profit Stop
REV   = Reverse Entry

- Chapter 22 -

UNLEADED GASOLINE

The New York Mercantile Exchange began trading Unleaded Gasoline futures in 1984 and options on these futures began trading in 1989. The size of the unleaded gasoline contract is 42,000 gallons. Gasoline is the major "cut" from a barrel of crude oil and accounts for nearly half of U. S. oil consumption.

Gasoline supplies are determined by the refineries' production. Gasoline is produced year-round to meet transportation demands. Due to the emphasis on heating oil production in the fall and winter, gasoline supplies can drop precipitously. Under normal conditions, this does not create a problem.

The demand for unleaded gasoline is twice that of the other petroleum products. The U. S. demand for gasoline is greatest during the summer vacation months. A poor economy, high unemployment and low consumer confidence can have a strong negative effect on exactly how great that demand will be.

The American Petroleum Institute (API) weekly reports are always important to the gasoline trader.

UNLEADED GASOLINE TRADE #1

Mega-Seasonals Unleaded Gasoline Trade #1 profits from the uptrend in Unleaded Gasoline from March through May. This is the time period that refineries switch their production emphasis from heating oil over to gasoline. Gasoline supplies are normally low at this time of the year and demand is beginning to increase. This leads to higher gasoline prices. The Unleaded Gasoline Trade #1 has made $18,226 in the last 12 years and has traded in every year.

PERFORMANCE HISTORY (1986-1997)

Total Profit...$18,226
Total Years Examined 12
Profit Years 9 (75%)
Loss Years 3 (25%)
Inactive Years 0
Average Profit.......................................$2,289
Average Loss $791
Profit-to-Loss Ratio 2.9
Total Profits/Total Losses............................ 8.7

JULY UNLEADED GASOLINE
1986 - 1997

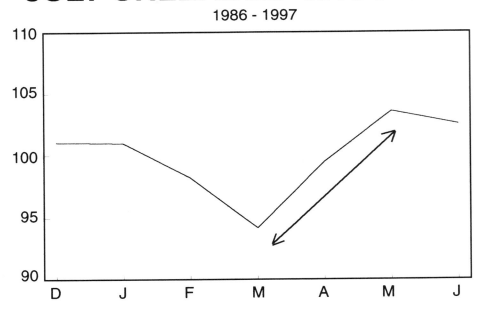

Rules for Unleaded Gasoline Trade #1

1. Enters long July Unleaded Gasoline from the first trading day of March through the last trading day of April.

2. Place a long entry stop 1 tick above the high of the last 18 trading days. Moving this stop as needed.

3. When your order is filled, place a protective sell stop 1 tick below the low of the last 4 trading days.

4. When the lowest low of the last 11 trading days is equal to or greater than your entry price, raise your sell stop to 1 tick below the low of the last 11 trading days. Raise this stop as needed.

5. Exit this trade on the close of the first trading day after May 12th.

Historical Results for Unleaded Gasoline Trade #1
July Unleaded Gasoline

HUN	ENTRY DATE	L/S	PRICE	EXIT DATE	EXIT METHOD	PRICE	TRADE P/L	YEARLY P/L
1986	04/23/86	L	4500	05/13/86	DATEX	5245	$ 3,129	$ 3,129
1987	03/09/87	L	5340	05/13/87	DATEX	5415	$ 315	$ 315
1988	03/21/88	L	4716	04/29/88	PSTOP	5040	$ 1,361	$ 1,361
1989	03/06/89	L	5376	05/05/89	PSTOP	6505	$ 4,742	$ 4,742
1990	03/28/90	L	6281	04/06/90	PROTS	6049	$ (974)	$ (974)
1991	03/04/91	L	6170	05/13/91	DATEX	6904	$ 3,083	$ 3,083
1992	03/13/92	L	6081	05/13/92	DATEX	6445	$ 1,529	$ 1,529
1993	03/04/93	L	6165	03/11/93	PROTS	6019	$ (613)	$ (613)
1994	03/21/94	L	4766	03/28/94	PROTS	4584	$ (764)	
	04/04/94	L	4796	05/13/94	DATEX	5171	$ 1,575	$ 811
1995	03/22/95	L	5711	05/15/95	DATEX	6227	$ 2,167	$ 2,167
1996	03/12/96	L	5731	05/13/96	DATEX	6555	$ 3,461	$ 3,461
1997	04/29/97	L	6141	05/02/97	PROTS	5954	$ (785)	$ (785)

TOTAL $ 18,226

Exit Legend:

DATEX = Exit Date
PROTS = Protective Stop
PSTOP = Profit Stop
REV   = Reverse Entry

- Chapter 23 -

VALUE LINE INDEX

The Kansas City Board of Trade was the first to trade futures on an equity index. The Value Line Index began trading on February 24, 1982. It is based on the Value Line Corporation's Arithmetic Index of 1650 stocks traded on the New York, the American, the Nasdaq and Canadian Exchanges. The contract value is $500 times the index price. The Value Line Index has a little brother, the Mini-Value Line Index. This Index is valued at $100 times the index price and was designed for the smaller trader. Options are traded on the "Mini-Value Line Index" but participation is presently quite low.

This equity index is all demand driven. It reflects the total expectations of all market participants. Prices rise or fall on the equity traders confidence in the economy and confidence in future economic trends.

The Value Line Index responds to the many reports issued by the U. S. Government. The reports that affect equities are also the reports that affect the interest rate markets. These two markets are normally joined at the wrists and move in tandem. Both the reports and the interest rate markets (T-Bonds, T-Notes, etc.) should be watched by the Value Line Index trader.

VALUE LINE INDEX TRADE #1

Mega-Seasonals Value Line Index Trade #1 is the well known equities "Summer Rally." The rally is fueled by declining interest rates and increasing investment funds from tax refunds. These increase the demand side of the equation and drive equities, and therefore indices, higher. The Value Line Index Trade #1 is backed up by the June Value Line Index Seasonal Chart below. The Value Line Index Trade #1 has made profits of $78,475 since 1982, with an average yearly loss of only $600!

PERFORMANCE HISTORY (1982-1997)

Total Profit $78,475
Total Years Examined 16
Profit Years 12 (75%)
Loss Years 4 (25%)
Inactive Years 0
Average Profit $6,740
Average Loss $600
Profit-to-Loss Ratio 11.2
Total Profits/Total Losses 33.7

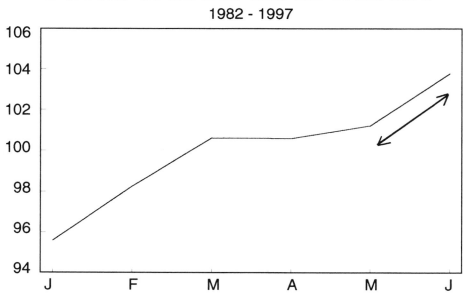

JUNE VALUE LINE INDEX
1982 - 1997

Rules for Value Line Index Trade #1:

1. Enters long June Value Line Index from the second trading day of May through the first trading day of June.

2. Place a long entry stop 5 points (1 tick) above the 5-day high. Change this as needed.

3. When filled, place a protective sell stop 5 points under the low of the last 4 trading days.

4. When the low of the last 12 trading days is equal to or greater than the entry price, raise the stop to 5 points under the 12 day low. Raise this stop as the 12 day low increases.

5. Exit trade on the close of the first trading day after June 3rd.

Historical Results for Value Line Index Trade #1
June Value Line

KVM	ENTRY DATE	L/S	PRICE	EXIT DATE	EXIT METHOD	PRICE	TRADE P/L	YEARLY P/L
1982	05/06/82	L	132.15	05/17/82	PROTS	130.20	$ (975)	$ (975)
1983	05/04/83	L	191.25	06/06/83	DATEX	201.85	$ 5,300	$ 5,300
1984	05/02/84	L	183.55	05/11/84	PROTS	179.95	$ (1,800)	
	06/01/84	L	172.35	06/04/84	DATEX	174.25	$ 950	$ (850)
1985	05/07/85	L	193.60	06/04/85	DATEX	200.00	$ 3,200	$ 3,200
1986	05/09/86	L	240.15	05/15/86	PROTS	235.85	$ (2,150)	
	05/22/86	L	239.65	06/04/86	DATEX	243.50	$ 1,925	$ (225)
1987	05/05/87	L	258.25	05/18/87	PROTS	252.35	$ (2,950)	
	05/26/87	L	256.50	06/04/87	DATEX	261.70	$ 2,600	$ (350)
1988	05/16/88	L	228.25	05/18/88	PROTS	222.15	$ (3,050)	
	05/26/88	L	222.75	06/06/88	DATEX	233.50	$ 5,375	$ 2,325
1989	05/02/89	L	277.60	06/05/89	DATEX	286.10	$ 4,250	$ 4,250
1990	05/02/90	L	271.05	06/04/90	DATEX	293.15	$ 11,050	$ 11,050
1991	05/09/91	L	308.05	05/10/91	PROTS	303.35	$ (2,350)	
	05/21/91	L	303.85	06/04/91	DATEX	316.05	$ 6,100	$ 3,750
1992	05/04/92	L	353.55	06/04/92	DATEX	357.00	$ 1,725	$ 1,725
1993	05/04/93	L	407.75	06/04/93	DATEX	418.35	$ 5,300	$ 5,300
1994	05/18/94	L	442.35	06/06/94	DATEX	453.70	$ 5,675	$ 5,675
1995	05/02/95	L	496.20	06/05/95	DATEX	511.70	$ 7,750	$ 7,750
1996	05/10/96	L	629.80	06/04/96	DATEX	641.20	$ 5,700	$ 5,700
1997	05/02/97	L	708.50	06/04/97	DATEX	758.20	$ 24,850	$ 24,850

TOTAL $ 78,475

Exit Legend:

DATEX = Date Exit
PROTS = Protective Stop
PSTOP = Profit Stop
REV   = Reverse Entry

VALUE LINE INDEX TRADE #2

The Value Line Index Trade #2 has the very best historical profit record of any of the Index trades in this time period. This is definitely one of my all time favorites! The Mega-Seasonal Value Line Index Trade #2 has traded in all of the last 16 years for a profit of $184,140 and a 5.6 to 1 profitable year to loss year ratio. Even the smaller trader can take advantage of this trade with a Mini-Value Line Contract. (Performance History is based on a full-sized Value Line Index Contract.)

PERFORMANCE HISTORY (1983-1998)

Total Profit	$184,140
Total Years Examined	16
Profit Years	12 (75%)
Loss Years	4 (25%)
Inactive Years	0
Average Profit	$16,324
Average Loss	$2,938
Profit-to-Loss Ratio	5.6
Total Profits/Total Losses	16.7

MARCH VALUE LINE INDEX
1983 - 1998

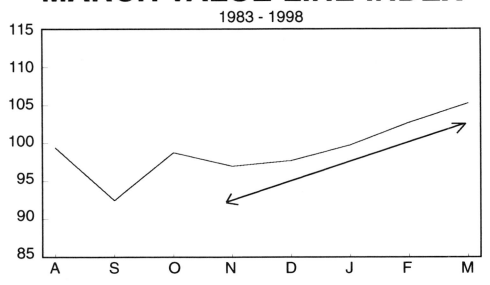

Rules for Value Line Index Trade #2:

1. Enters long March Value Line Index from the second trading day of November through the last trading day of January.

2. Place a long entry stop 5 points (1 tick) above the high of the last 12 days. Move this stop as necessary.

3. When filled, place a protective sell stop 5 points under the low of the last 2 trading days.

4. When the low of the last 30 trading days is equal to or greater than the entry price, move the stop up to 5 points under the 30 day low.

5. This trade does not have a fixed exit date. Keep moving the trailing stop in #4, until stopped out or the March Value Line goes off the board. Since this contract is settled for cash, your trade will be closed at the very last price.

Historical Results for Value Line Index Trade #2
March Value Line

KVH	ENTRY DATE	L/S	PRICE	EXIT DATE	EXIT METHOD	PRICE	TRADE P/L	YEARLY P/L
1983	11/03/82	L	155.15	03/31/83	DATEX	179.25	$ 12,050	$ 12,050
1984	11/11/83	L	195.95	02/03/84	PROTS	191.85	$ (2,050)	$ (2,050)
1985	12/18/84	L	181.00	03/11/85	PSTOP	195.80	$ 7,400	$ 7,400
1986	11/04/85	L	199.15	03/21/86	DATEX	241.45	$ 21,150	$ 21,150
1987	11/04/86	L	231.05	11/13/86	PROTS	226.55	$ (2,250)	
	12/02/86	L	231.75	12/29/86	PROTS	224.95	$ (3,400)	
	01/05/87	L	231.00	03/20/87	DATEX	273.20	$ 21,100	$ 15,450
1988	12/15/87	L	193.05	03/18/88	DATEX	233.80	$ 20,375	$ 20,375
1989	11/30/88	L	241.85	03/17/89	DATEX	261.20	$ 9,675	$ 9,675
1990	11/28/89	L	292.85	12/15/89	PROTS	291.00	$ (925)	
	01/02/90	L	298.05	01/10/90	PROTS	292.45	$ (2,800)	$ (3,725)
1991	11/09/90	L	227.00	01/14/91	PSTOP	230.10	$ 1,550	
	01/17/91	L	246.30	03/15/91	DATEX	294.65	$ 24,175	$ 25,725
1992	11/08/91	L	328.70	11/15/91	PROTS	322.95	$ (2,875)	
	12/23/91	L	315.75	03/20/92	DATEX	359.45	$ 21,850	$ 18,975
1993	11/05/92	L	360.30	03/19/93	DATEX	410.25	$ 24,975	$ 24,975
1994	11/02/93	L	452.05	11/02/93	PROTS	449.75	$ (1,150)	
	12/06/93	L	448.15	03/18/94	DATEX	476.75	$ 14,300	$ 13,150
1995	12/20/94	L	450.15	03/17/95	DATEX	473.55	$ 11,700	$ 11,700
1996	11/09/95	L	561.60	01/09/96	PSTOP	561.65	$ 25	
	01/26/96	L	573.45	03/08/96	PROTS	567.45	$ (3,000)	$ (2,975)
1997	11/12/96	L	671.55	03/21/97	DATEX	702.08	$ 15,265	$ 15,265
1998	12/01/97	L	887.05	12/10/97	PROTS	874.70	$ (6,175)	
	12/30/97	L	875.55	12/31/97	OPEN	881.90	$ 3,175	$ (3,000)

TOTAL $ 184,140

Exit Legend:

DATEX = Date Exit
PROTS = Protective Stop
PSTOP = Profit Stop
REV   = Reverse Entry

VALUE LINE INDEX TRADE #3

This is another version of the extended "Santa Claus Rally." I have included this trade for the smaller trader. It works superbly in the Mini-Value Line Contract. (The Performance History is based on the full-sized contract.) Like the other "Santa" trades, this is driven by the year-end window dressing of the fund managers. The seasonal chart for this trade shows how very strong this uptrend is. Mega-Seasonals Value Line Index Trade #3 has earned profits of $129,375 in the last 16 years traded and has been profitable in all but one year.

PERFORMANCE HISTORY (1983-1998)

Total Profit..$129,375
Total Years Examined 16
Profit Years 15 (94%)
Loss Years 1 (6%)
Inactive Years 0
Average Profit..$9,435
Average Loss $1,850
Profit-to-Loss Ratio 5.1
Total Profits/Total Losses...........................70.9

MARCH VALUE LINE INDEX
1983 - 1998

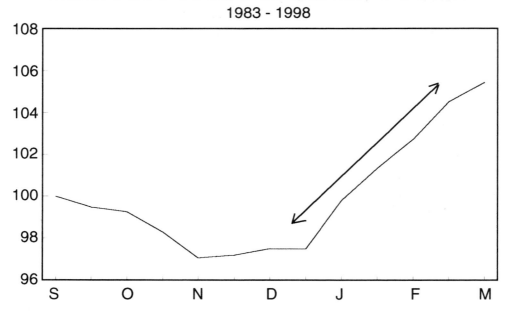

Rules for Value Line Index Trade #3:

1. Enters long March Value Line Index from December 15th through January 17th.

2. Place an entry stop 1 tick (5 points) above the 4-day high. Move this stop as needed.

3. When filled, place a protective sell stop 1 tick (5 points) under the 3-day low.

4. When the low of the last 5 trading days is equal to or greater than the entry price, move the stop up to 1 tick under the 5-day low. Raise this stop when necessary.

5. There is no set exit date on this trade. Continue raising the profit stop in #4 until stopped out or the March contract goes off the board. This contract is settled in cash, so your trade will be closed at the very last price.

174

Historical Results for Value Line Index Trade #3
March Value Line

KVH	ENTRY DATE	L/S	PRICE	EXIT DATE	EXIT METHOD	PRICE	TRADE P/L	YEARLY P/L
1983	12/21/82	L	155.90	01/03/83	PSTOP	158.55	$ 1,325	
	01/05/83	L	162.40	01/18/83	PSTOP	169.45	$ 3,525	$ 4,850
1984	12/21/83	L	196.35	01/16/84	PSTOP	202.20	$ 2,925	$ 2,925
1985	12/18/84	L	181.00	01/02/85	PSTOP	181.40	$ 200	
	01/09/85	L	183.20	02/20/85	PSTOP	200.50	$ 8,650	$ 8,850
1986	12/27/85	L	218.35	01/03/86	PROTS	213.35	$ (2,500)	
	01/06/86	L	220.65	01/09/86	PROTS	210.25	$ (5,200)	
	01/15/86	L	214.55	03/21/86	DATEX	241.45	$ 13,450	$ 5,750
1987	12/19/86	L	229.25	12/29/86	PROTS	226.45	$ (1,400)	
	01/05/87	L	231.00	01/22/87	PSTOP	244.40	$ 6,700	$ 5,300
1988	12/15/87	L	192.85	01/08/88	PSTOP	199.15	$ 3,150	
	01/15/88	L	211.00	03/18/88	DATEX	233.80	$ 11,400	$ 14,550
1989	12/19/88	L	244.75	01/03/89	PSTOP	246.25	$ 750	
	01/04/89	L	250.05	02/10/89	PSTOP	261.15	$ 5,550	$ 6,300
1990	12/26/89	L	291.50	01/09/90	PSTOP	295.05	$ 1,775	$ 1,775
1991	12/20/90	L	243.45	01/04/91	PROTS	239.75	$ (1,850)	
	01/16/91	L	235.25	02/26/91	PSTOP	283.65	$ 24,200	$ 22,350
1992	12/23/91	L	314.25	02/19/92	PSTOP	357.85	$ 21,800	$ 21,800
1993	12/17/92	L	379.35	01/08/93	PSTOP	382.95	$ 1,800	
	01/14/93	L	387.40	02/12/93	PSTOP	402.05	$ 7,325	$ 9,125
1994	12/17/93	L	450.05	01/24/94	PSTOP	461.85	$ 5,900	$ 5,900
1995	12/15/94	L	444.05	01/11/95	PSTOP	454.35	$ 5,150	$
	01/13/95	L	460.25	02/21/95	PSTOP	468.10	$ 3,925	$ 9,075
1996	12/21/95	L	575.55	01/09/96	PROTS	561.65	$ (6,950)	
	01/17/96	L	562.25	02/16/96	PSTOP	587.45	$ 12,600	$ 5,650
1997	12/19/96	L	683.00	01/10/97	PSTOP	685.00	$ 1,000	
	01/13/97	L	701.00	02/21/97	PSTOP	713.05	$ 6,025	$ 7,025
1998	12/17/97	L	875.00	12/19/97	PROTS	855.95	$ (9,525)	
	12/29/97	L	866.55	12/31/97	OPEN	881.90	$ 7,675	$ (1,850)

TOTAL $129,375

Exit Legend:

DATEX = Date Exit
PROTS = Protective Stop
PSTOP = Profit Stop
REV   = Reverse Entry

- Chapter 24 -

JAPANESE YEN

Futures on the Japanese Currency, the Yen, began trading on the International Monetary Market Division of the Chicago Mercantile Exchange in 1972. Options trading of the Yen Futures began in 1985. The IMM contract is 12.5 million Yen. The MidAmerica Commodity Exchange trades a 6.25 million Yen contract.

The Yen is mostly a demand driven market. The U. S./Japan Balance of Payments is extremely important in the determination of the price of the Yen versus the U. S. Dollar.

The Balance of Payments has two components. The first component, the Balance of Trade, is the difference between Japan's exports to the United States and Japan's imports from the United States. For quite a while the Japanese have had a positive balance of trade with the United States.

The second component of the Balance of Payments is the Flow of Capital. The Flow of Capital represents the movement of funds for investment purposes. Interest rate differentials and investment opportunities cause capital to flow from one country to another. The currency of the country with the lesser investment return must be converted into the currency of the country with the better investment return.

The economic situation in Japan has a direct effect on the price of the Yen. From time to time, the Japanese Central Bank, the Bank of Japan, will determine that the Yen/Dollar relationship is out of line and decide to halt the current trend by entering the currency markets to buy or sell the Yen. This consolidates the price of the Yen for a short time. The Yen normally resumes the previous trend.

All economic and interest rate reports of the U. S. and of Japan are important when trading the Yen. Especially significant are the results from the G7 meetings. These results have been know to redirect the market.

JAPANESE YEN TRADE #1

Looking at the June Yen Seasonal Chart, you can see a strong seasonal upmove in December. Immediately following is an equally strong downmove in January. However, if you look at the two directional seasonal charts on the next page, you see quite a different picture. In both charts it's the movement after mid-December through mid-January that provides the June Yen's trend until May. This indecision is a reaction to the Balance of Trade Report. Mega-Seasonals Japanese Yen Trade #1 enters either side of the market. This has been an excellent trade, earning a profit of $81,713 since 1977 with 90% of the years profitable.

PERFORMANCE HISTORY (1977-1997)

Total Profit $81,713
Total Years Examined 21
Profit Years 19 (90%)
Loss Years 2 (10%)
Inactive Years 0
Average Profit $4,447
Average Loss $1,395
Profit-to-Loss Ratio 3.2
Total Profits/Total Losses 30.3

JUNE YEN
1977 - 1997

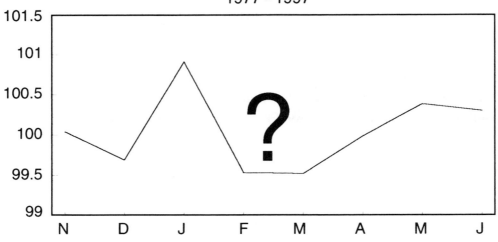

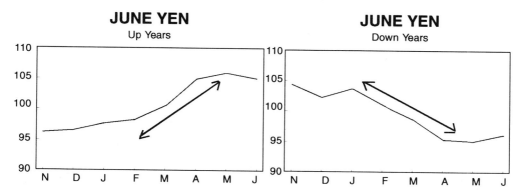

JUNE YEN
Up Years

JUNE YEN
Down Years

Rules for Japanese Yen Trade #1:

1. Enters long and short June Yen from the second trading day of February through March 21st.

2. Place a long entry stop 7 ticks above the high of the last 22 trading days and place a short entry stop 7 ticks below the low of the last 22 trading days. Continue moving these entry stops as needed.

3. When filled:
   On long: Place a protective sell stop 1 tick under the 6-day low.
   On short: Place a protective buy stop 1 tick above the 6-day high.

   Remember to continue entering the opposite entry order as described in #2 until you are no longer in the trade entry window. Should you already have entered a trade via #2 and the reverse entry price is greater than either your protective sell stop or profit stop (for longs), use the entry price to exit the current trade so that your new position is short. Of course, should you presently be short, adjust the protective buy stop or profit stop.

4. If long: When the low of the last 22 trading days is equal to or greater than your long entry price, raise your stop to 1 tick below the 22 day low.
   If short: When the high of the last 22 trading days is equal to or less than your short entry price, lower your stop to 1 tick above the 22 day high.

5. Exit trade on the close of the first trading day after April 14th.

Historical Results for Japanese Yen Trade #1
June Yen

JYM	ENTRY DATE	L/S	PRICE	EXIT DATE	EXIT METHOD	PRICE	TRADE P/L	YEARLY P/L
1977	02/08/77	L	3476	04/15/77	DATEX	3645	$ 2,113	$ 2,113
1978	02/17/78	L	4224	04/17/78	DATEX	4553	$ 3,863	$ 3,863
1979	02/28/79	S	5037	04/16/79	DATEX	4641	$ 4,950	$ 4,950
1980	02/08/80	S	4217	04/15/80	DATEX	3987	$ 2,875	$ 2,875
1981	02/13/81	S	4968	04/15/81	DATEX	4678	$ 3,625	$ 3,625
1982	02/02/82	S	4425	04/15/82	DATEX	4083	$ 4,275	$ 4,275
1983	02/02/83	S	4177	02/15/83	PROTS	4336	$ (1,988)	
	03/17/83	S	4193	04/15/83	DATEX	4228	$ (438)	$ (2,426)
1984	03/02/84	L	4364	04/16/84	DATEX	4471	$ 1,338	$ 1,338
1985	02/04/85	S	3899	03/19/85	REV	3954	$ (688)	
	03/19/85	L	3954	04/15/85	DATEX	4018	$ 800	$ 112
1986	02/05/86	L	5285	04/07/86	PSTOP	5523	$ 2,975	$ 2,975
1987	03/16/87	L	6633	04/15/87	DATEX	7087	$ 5,675	$ 5,675
1988	03/11/88	L	7918	04/15/88	DATEX	8113	$ 2,438	$ 2,438
1989	02/15/89	L	8070	03/10/89	PROTS	7845	$ (2,813)	
	03/10/89	S	7839	04/17/89	DATEX	7643	$ 2,450	$ (363)
1990	02/22/90	S	6848	04/16/90	DATEX	6287	$ 7,013	$ 7,013
1991	02/04/91	L	7622	02/25/91	PROTS	7505	$ (1,463)	
	02/25/91	S	7499	04/09/91	PSTOP	7361	$ 1,725	$ 262
1992	02/20/92	S	7745	04/08/92	PSTOP	7577	$ 2,100	$ 2,100
1993	02/09/93	L	8176	04/15/93	DATEX	8832	$ 8,200	$ 8,200
1994	02/11/94	L	9345	04/15/94	DATEX	9688	$ 4,288	$ 4,288
1995	02/16/95	L	10360	04/17/95	DATEX	12288	$ 24,100	$ 24,100
1996	02/20/96	L	9719	03/19/96	REV	9514	$ (2,563)	
	03/19/96	S	9514	04/16/96	DATEX	9291	$ 2,788	$ 225
1997	02/04/97	S	8329	04/15/97	DATEX	8003	$ 4,075	$ 4,075

TOTAL $ 81,713

Exit Legend:

DATEX = Exit Date
PROTS = Protective Stop
PSTOP = Profit Stop
REV   = Reverse Entry

MEGA-SEASONALS
"ENTRY TYPE" CALENDAR

FUTURE	PAGE #	J	F	M	A	M	J	J	A	S	O	N	D
T-Bonds #1	30	B	B										
Cocoa #1	44	S											
T-Notes #1	128	B	B										
Lumber #1	114		S	S									
Japanese Yen #1	176		B	B									
Crude Oil #1	78			L	L								
Heating Oil #1	100			L	L								
Live Hogs #1	110			L	L	L							
Unleaded Gas #1	162			L	L								
D-Mark #1	86				S	S	S						
Pork Bellies #1	136				S	S	S						
T-Bonds #2	33					L	L						
Copper #1	58					B	B	B					
Corn #1	66					S	S	S					
NYSE Index #1	118					L	L						
T-Notes #2	131					L	L						
S&P Index #1	144					L	L						
Soybeans #1	154					S	S	S					
Soybean Oil #1	158					S	S	S					
Value Line #1	166					L	L						
Coffee #1	48						S	S	S				
Cotton #1	70						S	S					
D-Mark #2	89						B	B					
Pork Bellies #2	139						L	L					
Heating Oil #2	103							L	L	L			
Coffee #2	51							L	L				
Crude Oil #2	81							L	L				
T-Bonds #3	36								L	L	L		
Coffee #3	54								S	S			
Copper #2	61	L										L	L
D-Mark #3	92	S										S	S
Heating Oil #3	106	S										S	S
NYSE Index #2	121	L										L	L
S&P Index #2	147	L										L	L
Value Line #2	169	L										L	L
Live Cattle #1	40	L											L
Cotton #2	73												B
Gold #1	96	S	S	S									S
NYSE Index #3	124	L											L
S&P Index #3	150	L											L
Value Line #3	172	L											L
		J̄	F̄	M̄	Ā	M̄	J̄	J̄	Ā	S̄	Ō	N̄	D̄

L = Long   S = Short   B = Both Long And Short

TRADE CALENDAR OF ENTRY WINDOWS

182

MAY
New:

T-Bonds #2	33	S&P Index #1	144
Copper #1	58	Soybeans #1	154
Corn #1	66	Soybean Oil #1	158
NYSE Index #1	118	V. L. Index #1	166
T-Notes #2	131		

Continuing:

D-Mark #1	86	Pork Bellies #1	136
Live Hogs #1	110		

JUNE
New:

Coffee #1	48	D-Mark #2	89
Cotton #1	70	Pork Bellies #2	139

Continuing:

T-Bonds #2	33	Pork Bellies #1	136
Copper #1	58	S&P Index #1	144
Corn #1	66	Soybeans #1	154
D-Mark #1	86	Soybean Oil #1	158
NYSE Index #1	118	V. L. Index #1	166
T-Notes #2	131		

JULY
New:

Heating Oil #2	103

Continuing:

Coffee #1	48	D-Mark #2	89
Copper #1	58	Pork Bellies #2	139
Corn #1	66	Soybeans #1	154
Cotton #1	70	Soybean Oil #1	158

AUGUST
New:

Coffee #2	51	Crude Oil #2	81

Continuing:

Coffee #1	48	Heating Oil #2	103

SEPTEMBER
New:

T-Bonds #3	36	Coffee #3	54

Continuing:

Coffee #2	51	Heating Oil #2	103
Crude Oil #2	81		

OCTOBER
New: None

Continuing:

T-Bonds #3	36	Coffee #3	54

NOVEMBER
New:

Copper #2	61	NYSE Index #2	121
D-Mark #3	92	S&P Index #2	147
Heating Oil #3	106	V. L. Index #2	169

Continuing:

T-Bonds #3	36

DECEMBER
New:

Live Cattle #1	40	NYSE Index #3	124
Cotton #2	73	S&P Index #3	150
Gold #1	96	V. L. Index #3	172

Continuing:

Copper #2	61	NYSE Index #2	124
D-Mark #3	92	S&P Index #2	147
Heating Oil #3	106	V. L. Index #2	169

BIBLIOGRAPHY

1. L. R. Williams and M. L. Noseworthy, Sure Thing Commodity Trading, Windsor Books, Brightwaters, New York, 1977.

2. Evert H. Beckner, Techni-Seasonal Commodity Trading, Windsor Books, Brightwaters, New York, 1984.

3. Richard J. Teweles, Charles V. Harlow and Herbert L. Stone, The Commodity Futures Game, McGraw-Hill Book Company, New York, New York, 1974.

4. Yale Hirsch, Stock Traders Almanac, The Hirsch Organization, Inc., Old Tappan, New Jersey.